By Marc Schindler

Copyright 2019 Marc Schindler. All rights reserved.

No part of this book may be reproduced in any form or by any electronic or mechanical means, including information storage and retrieval systems, without permission in writing from the publisher. The only exception is by a reviewer, who may quote short excerpts in a published review.

Published by Marc Schindler Publishing

Cover design by Marc Schindler.

ISBN PAPERBACK: 9798320558462

The information presented herein represents the view of the author as of the date of publication. This book is presented for informational purposes only. Due to the rate at which conditions change, the author reserves the right to alter and update his opinions based on new conditions. While every attempt has been made to verify the information in this book, neither the author nor his affiliates/partners assume any responsibility for errors, inaccuracies, or omissions.

Introduction	4
The allure of the Big 4 in London	4
The Job Seeker's Perspective	5
Overview of the Big 4 hiring landscape in London	7
Chapter 1: Knowing the Big 4	10
Understanding the Big 4	10
Services and sectors covered by the Big 4	11
Culture and values of the Big 4 firms	12
Culture and values: The reality	14
The Hiring Process	15
Chapter 2: Preparing Your Application	18
Tailoring Your CV for the Big 4	18
10 steps to customise your CV:	19
Crafting a standout cover letter	24
Essential Qualifications and Certifications	27
Chapter 3: Networking	32
Networking Strategies	34
The 3 types of networking	43
Chapter 4 – Acing the Interview	48
Understanding the Firm's Core Values	49
Crafting Your Personal Narratives	51
Tailoring Stories to Different Themes	53
Practicing Your Delivery	55
The initial interviews	56
The technical interview	60
Aligning Personal Goals with Firm's Objectives	63
Chapter 5: Cultural Adaptation	65
Mastering British Workplace Norms	66
Effective communication and teamwork in a diverse environment	67
Understanding Diversity in the Big Four	67

Developing Effective Communication Skills	71
Practical Tips for Thriving in a Diverse Team at a Big Four Firm	72
Flexibility and Adaptability	73
Chapter 6: Career Growth and Development	76
Long-term Career Paths within the Big 4	76
Pursuing Further Education and Certifications	79
Other Technology-Related Qualifications	81
Leadership Development Programs	82
Leadership Roles in Projects	85
International Assignments	85
Conclusion	87
Afterword	88

Introduction

Hey there! I'm the author of "London Calling: Unlocking the doors at the Big 4," and let me tell you, it's been quite the journey putting this book together. You see, I've always been passionate about helping folks build meaningful careers, and nothing gets me more excited than seeing someone land their dream job. That's exactly why I wrote this book.

I remember starting out in my own career, feeling a bit lost and wishing I had a guide to navigate the complex world of job hunting, especially one as competitive as the Big 4 in London. So, I decided to be that guide for others. This book is packed with all the insider tips and strategies I've learned over the years, tailored specifically for professionals with the ambition to break into the Big 4. It's like having a friend in the biz who's got your back.

My goal? To empower you with the knowledge and confidence to not just land a job, but to thrive in it. I've poured my heart into these pages, sharing personal anecdotes and easy-to-follow advice because I believe everyone deserves a shot at their dream role. And let's be real, who doesn't want to work in one of the most dynamic cities in the world?

So, whether you're fresh out of college or looking to make a big career move, this book is your roadmap to success. It's not just about getting a job; it's about building a career that makes you jump out of bed every morning, excited for the day ahead. And trust me, if I can do it, so can you. Let's turn those aspirations into achievements together! 🚀

The allure of the Big 4 in London

The allure of the Big 4 accounting firms in London is multifaceted, drawing professionals from across the globe, particularly from India. The Big 4—Deloitte, PricewaterhouseCoopers (PwC), Ernst & Young (EY), and KPMG—represent the pinnacle of professional achievement in accounting and consulting. Their London offices are not just at the heart of global finance but also stand as beacons of career advancement and professional development.

> IN 2023, THE BIG 4 FIRMS COLLECTIVELY EMPLOYED MORE THAN 1.5 MILLION PEOPLE WORLDWIDE1. DELOITTE HAD THE LARGEST WORKFORCE WITH APPROXIMATELY 457,000 EMPLOYEES, FOLLOWED BY EY, PWC, AND KPMG.
>
> IN THE UK, AS OF THE FOURTH QUARTER OF 2022, THERE WERE 6.2 MILLION FOREIGN-BORN PEOPLE EMPLOYED, MAKING UP NEARLY A FIFTH OF THE WORKING POPULATION

For professionals, the Big 4 in London offer an unparalleled opportunity to work on complex, high-profile projects with some of the world's most prestigious clients. The experience gained in such an environment is invaluable, providing exposure to innovative practices and international business strategies. Moreover, working in London allows for a unique blend of professional rigor and cultural diversity, which is highly appealing to those seeking to broaden their horizons.

The reputation of the Big 4 as career accelerators is another significant draw. They are known for their rigorous training programs, mentorship opportunities, and a clear path for career progression. Ambitious individuals see these firms as a platform to catapult their careers to new heights, with the potential for roles in leadership and opportunities to work abroad.

Additionally, the Big 4 in London are at the forefront of innovation in professional services, from advancements in financial technology to sustainability consulting. For professionals who are eager to be part of a dynamic and evolving industry, the Big 4 offer a chance to be at the forefront of change and to make a tangible impact on the future of business.

Lastly, the lifestyle and prestige associated with living and working in one of the world's most vibrant cities cannot be understated. London's status as a global hub for finance, culture, and education adds to the allure, making a position at the Big 4 not just a job, but a gateway to a world of possibilities. For many, the dream of working at the Big 4 in London is not just about professional growth, but also about the life-changing experiences that come with it.

The Job Seeker's Perspective

Understanding the international job seeker's perspective, especially when it comes to securing a position in the Big 4 in London, requires a deep dive into the unique challenges and aspirations that define this demographic. International professionals often view the Big 4 as not just employers but as gateways to global exposure, professional growth, and financial stability. The prestige associated with these firms is highly coveted, and the opportunity to work in a cosmopolitan city like London is seen as a career milestone.

The educational background of international job seekers is typically robust, with many holding degrees from prestigious universities. However, they often face the challenge of translating their qualifications and experience to meet the expectations of the Big 4 in London. This includes understanding the nuances of the Western corporate culture, refining communication skills, and navigating the complexities of work visa regulations. There's a strong desire to align their skillset with international standards, which often means pursuing additional certifications or training.

Another aspect is the competitive nature of the job market. International job seekers are well aware that they are competing against a global talent pool. This drives them to seek out every possible advantage, from acquiring specialized knowledge in fields like SAP consulting to developing a strong personal brand. Networking plays a crucial role in this, as does the ability to showcase one's achievements and potential impact to prospective employers.

> INDIAN TERTIARY EDUCATION HAS SEEN SIGNIFICANT GROWTH AND DIVERSIFICATION, SETTING A STRONG FOUNDATION FOR JOB SEEKERS AIMING FOR CAREERS IN GLOBAL MARKETS LIKE THE BIG 4 IN LONDON. HERE ARE SOME STATISTICS THAT HIGHLIGHT THE CURRENT LANDSCAPE: ENROLMENT: THE TOTAL ENROLMENT IN HIGHER EDUCATION IN INDIA REACHED NEARLY 4.14 CRORE IN 2020-21, UP FROM 3.85 CRORE IN 2019-201. FEMALE ENROLMENT: THE NUMBER OF FEMALE STUDENTS ENROLLED IN HIGHER EDUCATION INCREASED TO 2.01 CRORE FROM 1.88 CRORE IN 2019-20, WITH THE PERCENTAGE OF FEMALE ENROLMENT TO TOTAL ENROLMENT RISING FROM 45% IN 2014-15 TO AROUND 49% IN 2020-211. INSTITUTIONS: INDIA'S HIGHER EDUCATION LANDSCAPE IS VAST, WITH 1,043 UNIVERSITIES, 42,343 COLLEGES, AND 11,779 STAND-ALONE INSTITUTIONS, MAKING IT ONE OF THE LARGEST HIGHER EDUCATION SECTORS IN THE WORLD2. GLOBAL RANKING: INDIAN INSTITUTES LIKE IIT MADRAS HAVE BEEN RECOGNIZED AS LEADING INSTITUTIONS FOR ENGINEERING, REFLECTING THE QUALITY OF EDUCATION THAT INTERNATIONAL JOB SEEKERS BRING TO THE INTERNATIONAL JOB MARKET. EDUCATION EXPENDITURE: THE INDIAN GOVERNMENT'S EXPENDITURE ON THE EDUCATION SECTOR SAW AN INCREASE OF ALMOST 12 PERCENT IN 2023 COMPARED TO THE PREVIOUS YEAR, INDICATING A STRONG COMMITMENT TO ENHANCING EDUCATIONAL INFRASTRUCTURE."

The motivation to relocate to London also stems from personal aspirations. For many International professionals, working in London represents a blend of professional opportunity and life experience. They are drawn to the city's rich cultural tapestry, its history, and the chance to experience life in one of the world's most influential cities. This personal dimension often fuels their job-seeking efforts, adding a layer of passion and determination to their applications.

Financial considerations are also significant. The Big 4 in London offer competitive salaries and benefits, which are attractive to International job seekers looking to support families back home or to save for the future. The potential for career advancement and the subsequent financial rewards are strong incentives that drive their ambition and willingness to adapt to new environments.

Lastly, there's a sense of pride and accomplishment that comes with breaking into the Big 4 in London. For international job seekers, it's not just about the job itself; it's about the affirmation of their professional capabilities on a global stage. It's a testament to their hard work, perseverance, and the sacrifices they've made along the way. This emotional component is a powerful force in their journey towards securing their dream job in the Big 4.

Overview of the Big 4 hiring landscape in London

D. Deloitte 4.0 ★

Senior Consultant , Android Developer, Deloitte Digital

London, England

GBP 42K - 60K (Glassdoor Est.)

You'll have all the support you need to succeed, including robust tech and home workstation set-up guidance, as well as access to a variety of flexible working...... 30d+

D. Deloitte 4.0 ★

Assistant Director, Corporate Turnaround, Performance Improvement, Financial Advisor

London, England

Leading certain aspects of the team's marketing and business development activities to develop and convert our sales pipeline;... 30d+

D. Deloitte 4.0 ★

Consultant, International Pensions Tax

London, England

GBP 42K - 60K (Glassdoor Est.)

Location: The home office of this role is London with occasional domestic and international travel. Assisting large global clients in coordinating large scale...... 30d+

The Big 4—Deloitte, PwC, EY, and KPMG—represent the zenith of the accounting and consulting world, particularly in the influential financial hub of London. These firms are not just powerhouses in the financial industry; they are also among the most sought-after employers for professionals seeking to ascend in their careers. The hiring landscape within these organizations is fiercely competitive, reflecting the ambitious standards and expectations that are synonymous with their global reputation.

Recruitment Trends and Statistics The Big 4 recruit throughout the year, with a significant intake of new hires starting in September. They offer a range of internships and graduate programs across advisory, audit, tax, consulting, and technology, attracting a diverse pool of candidates. For example, KPMG's graduate scheme, which is one of the common routes into the firm, offers a starting salary of approximately £34,500 per year for those working towards becoming chartered accountants.

Salary Progression Working for the Big 4 is an aspiration for many due to the professional growth it promises and the potential for salary progression. An entry-level auditor at Deloitte in the UK can expect to earn around £30,000 per year initially, with the potential to earn more than £45,000 per annum as a chartered accountant. This progression is closely tied to performance, with the possibility of raises and promotions for those who positively impact their department and the firm.

Challenges and Opportunities The recruitment process is multi-stage and exhaustive, designed to identify candidates who can thrive in a demanding and dynamic environment. The initial applications are online, followed by a series of assessments tailored to the specific business area the candidate has applied for. This rigorous selection process ensures that only the most capable and adaptable individuals join the ranks of these esteemed firms.

AUDIT DIVISION THE AUDIT DIVISION IS A CRITICAL COMPONENT OF THE BIG 4, WITH DELOITTE LEADING THE CHARGE IN REVENUE FROM ITS ASSURANCE SEGMENT, GENERATING APPROXIMATELY $20.1 BILLION IN 20233. THE BIG 4 SERVE AS AUDITORS TO THE MAJORITY OF PUBLICLY TRADED COMPANIES AND ALSO DEAL WITH A NUMBER OF PRIVATE COMPANIES, MAKING THEM INFLUENTIAL PLAYERS IN THE AUDIT SECTOR.

TAX DIVISION IN THE TAX DIVISION, THE BIG 4 HAVE DEMONSTRATED THEIR PROWESS WITH DELOITTE GENERATING AROUND $10.3 BILLION, PWC WITH $11.77 BILLION, EY WITH $12.1 BILLION, AND KPMG WITH $7.9 BILLION IN REVENUE FROM THEIR TAX SERVICES IN 20233. THESE FIRMS ARE KNOWN FOR THEIR TAX ADVISORY SERVICES AND HAVE A SIGNIFICANT IMPACT ON TAX PRACTICES GLOBALLY.

CONSULTING DIVISION THE CONSULTING BRANCHES OF THE BIG 4 ARE AMONG THE TEN LARGEST CONSULTING FIRMS BY REVENUE. THEY OUTDO OTHER MANAGEMENT CONSULTING FIRMS IN TERMS OF EMPLOYEE AND OFFICE NUMBERS, EACH BOASTING AROUND 600-800 OFFICES AND 200,000-300,000 EMPLOYEES GLOBALLY. IN TERMS OF REVENUE, DELOITTE'S ADVISORY/CONSULTING SEGMENT GENERATED APPROXIMATELY $29.6 BILLION, INDICATING THE SCALE AND SCOPE OF THEIR CONSULTING OPERATIONS.

Diversity and Inclusion In recent years, the Big 4 have made concerted efforts to diversify their workforce. EY, for example, has implemented a policy where no applications are screened out based solely on A-level or degree grades, focusing instead on the scores obtained during online assessments1. This shift reflects a broader trend within the industry to create more inclusive work environments and provide equal opportunities for all candidates, regardless of their educational background.

Impact of COVID-19 The COVID-19 pandemic has brought about significant changes in the hiring processes of the Big 4, with many aspects of recruitment and onboarding going virtual. KPMG, for instance, had to adapt its recruitment for the class of 2021 to a fully virtual format, including virtual assessment centers. This transition to digital has allowed the Big 4 to maintain their recruitment activities even amidst the challenges posed by the pandemic.

Chapter 1: Knowing the Big 4

Understanding the Big 4

The Big 4 accounting firms—Deloitte, PricewaterhouseCoopers (PwC), Ernst & Young (EY), and KPMG—are the titans of the professional services industry. They are not only the largest global accounting networks by revenue but also the most prestigious, offering a wide array of services that extend far beyond traditional accounting. These services include audit, assurance, taxation, management consulting, actuarial, corporate finance, and legal services[1].

The Big 4 have a storied history, with roots that intertwine with the very fabric of modern business practices. Their origins date back to the 19th century, and over time, they have evolved through a series of mergers and expansions to dominate the market. Today, they are known for setting the standards in accounting and auditing, influencing regulations, and shaping the industry's future through innovation and thought leadership.

With operations in over 150 countries, the Big 4 employ hundreds of thousands of professionals worldwide. They are responsible for auditing a significant majority of public companies, as well as many private companies, which underscores their influence on global financial practices[1]. Their global reach allows them to provide consistent and comprehensive services to multinational clients, making them indispensable partners in global commerce.

In London, the Big 4's significance is particularly pronounced. They audit 99% of the companies in the FTSE 100 Index and 96% of the companies in the FTSE 250 Index, reflecting their dominance in one of the world's leading financial centers[1]. Their role in London not only contributes to the city's economic stability but also to its reputation as a global hub for finance and business.

Each of the Big 4 is not a single firm but a network of independent firms that have agreed to adhere to common quality standards and share a brand and intellectual property. This structure allows them to be agile and responsive to the specific regulatory environments of the various countries in which they operate. As a job seeker, this enables you to access a world of opportunities across different countries and business environments and allows for diverse career paths within the same organization. You might start in one country or service line and then transfer to another, leveraging the firm's global reach to shape your career trajectory. The Big 4's global presence means you could work in various jurisdictions while benefiting from the firms' ability to adapt to local regulations and cultures. This can be particularly advantageous for those looking to gain international experience

Despite the geographical spread, the Big 4 maintain consistent quality standards and practices across their network. This ensures that employees can expect a uniform professional experience, with the added benefit of a recognizable and respected brand name on their resume.

The Big 4's primary sources of revenue have traditionally been from their audit and assurance services. However, in recent years, consulting has become increasingly profitable, with some firms reporting that consulting revenue has surpassed that of auditing. This shift reflects the changing landscape of business needs and the Big 4's adaptability to meet those needs.

> I WAS A SENIOR DIRECTOR IN CONSULTING, SPECIALISING IN SAP TRANSFORMATION PROJECTS. THE STRUCTURE OF THE SAP DIVISION IS REPRESENTATIVE OF THE STRUCTURE OF ALL THE OTHER DIVISIONS, WHETHER ORACLE, FINANCIAL ADVISORY, RISK ADVISORY AND SO ON.
>
> EACH DIVISION CONSISTS OF A MARKET OFFERING, SUCH AS ENTERPRISE TRANSFORMATION, WHICH IN TURN IS BROKEN DOWN INTO GO-TO MARKETS. FOR ET, IT WAS SPLIT INTO FINANCE, CUSTOMER, SUPPLY CHAIN AND ANALYTICS. THE GTMS ARE LEAD BY SENIOR MANAGERS OR DIRECTORS AND IS FURTHER SUB-DIVIDED INTO CAPABILITIES. EACH CAPABILITY IS LED BY A SENIOR MANAGER OR MANAGER. OVER AND ABOVE YOUR PROJECT WORK, YOU WILL HAVE PRACTICE DEVELOPMENT (PD) GOALS, GEARED TOWARDS ACHIEVING THE OVERALL MO OBJECTIVES.

Despite their success, the Big 4 face challenges, including concerns over market dominance and potential conflicts of interest due to their multifaceted services. These concerns have led to calls for increased regulation and oversight to ensure the integrity of the financial markets.

In summary, the Big 4 accounting firms are more than just auditors; they are integral components of the global financial system. Their expertise, resources, and global presence enable them to serve clients across a spectrum of industries, helping to navigate the complexities of modern business and finance. The Big 4's history, development, and current operations underscore their pivotal role in shaping the economic landscape of today and tomorrow.

Services and sectors covered by the Big 4

Audit and Assurance Services At their core, the Big 4 provide audit and assurance services, which remain a cornerstone of their operations. They conduct a significant majority of the audits for public companies, as well as many private companies, ensuring the accuracy and reliability of financial reporting. This function is critical for maintaining investor confidence and the proper functioning of capital markets.

Taxation and Legal Services Taxation services are another key offering, with the Big 4 providing expert advice on tax planning, compliance, and controversy. They help businesses navigate the complexities of multiple tax jurisdictions and changing regulations. Additionally, they offer a range of legal services, assisting clients with corporate law, mergers and acquisitions, and regulatory compliance.

Consulting and Advisory Services The consulting and advisory arms of the Big 4 have seen substantial growth, advising clients on a variety of issues including strategy, operations, technology, and human resources. These services are designed to improve clients' business performance, manage risk, and transform operations to better compete in a rapidly changing environment.

Specialized Services Beyond these core areas, the Big 4 also provide specialized services such as actuarial, valuation, and market research. They help companies assess risks, value assets, and understand market dynamics to make informed business decisions. Their expertise in these niche areas is supported by deep industry knowledge and analytical capabilities.

Sector Coverage In terms of sector coverage, the Big 4 serve a wide range of industries, from financial services and technology to healthcare and energy. They tailor their services to meet the unique challenges of each sector, leveraging their global network and industry-specific expertise to deliver solutions that address the specific needs of their clients.

Culture and values of the Big 4 firms

The culture and values of the Big 4 accounting firms—Deloitte, PwC, EY, and KPMG—are foundational to their identity and operations. These values not only define the internal environment of each firm but also shape their interactions with clients and the broader community.

Commitment to Integrity and Ethics At the heart of the Big 4's culture is a strong commitment to integrity and ethics. They emphasize the importance of doing the right thing, even when no one is watching. This commitment is reflected in their rigorous compliance with auditing standards and regulations, and their dedication to transparency and honesty in all business dealings.

ITS NOT PERFECT...

ALTHOUGH THESE VALUES SHOULD NOT BE JUST ABSTRACT CONCEPTS AND THEY SHOULD BE LIVED DAILY BY THE EMPLOYEES OF THE BIG 4, THESE FIRMS ARE EXTREMELY COMPETITIVE IN NATURE, AND THAT COMPETITIVENESS SEEPS INTO THE DAILY CULTURE. IT CAN BE CUT-THROAT. YOU ARE CONSTANTLY REMINDED THAT YOUR USEFULNESS TO THE FIRM IS DEPENDENT ON YOUR CONTRIBUTIONS TO PROFIT OR OTHER OUTPUTS. YOUR BILLABLE TARGETS ARE HIGH. YOU HAVE DEMANDING PD DELIVERABLES AND YOU WILL BE JUDGED BY THESE OUTPUTS, THAT DETERMINE YOUR BONUS AND INCREASES. UNFORTUNATELY, PERSONALITIES DO CLASH. YOU

ARE REPRESENTED BY YOUR PEOPLE LEADER IN PERFORMANCE MEETINGS. IF YOU AND YOUR PL DO NOT GET ALONG, OR HE IS NOT A STRONG SUPPORTER OF YOUR CAREER, IT COULD NEGATIVELY IMPACT YOUR PROGRESSION. ALTERNATIVELY, IF YOU CLASH WITH A LEADER ON A PROJECT, NEGATIVE FEEDBACK DOES HURT AND THE FEEDBACK MAY NOT ALWAYS BE OBJECTIVE.

Focus on Excellence and Quality The Big 4 firms strive for excellence and quality in their services. They are known for their meticulous attention to detail and the high standards they set for their work. This pursuit of excellence is ingrained in their employees from day one, fostering a culture of continuous improvement and professional growth.

Inclusivity and Diversity Inclusivity and diversity are key components of the Big 4's culture. They recognize the value of diverse perspectives and experiences and are committed to creating an inclusive environment where all employees can thrive. This commitment extends to their hiring practices, professional development programs, and community engagement initiatives.

Innovation and Adaptability The Big 4 firms value innovation and adaptability, understanding that the business landscape is constantly evolving. They encourage their employees to think creatively, embrace modern technologies, and adapt to changing market conditions. This culture of innovation allows them to stay ahead of industry trends and meet the complex needs of their clients.

Collaboration and Teamwork Collaboration and teamwork are central to the Big 4's approach to service delivery. They foster a collaborative environment where professionals from various disciplines work together to solve complex problems. This teamwork extends beyond individual firms, as the Big 4 often collaborate with each other on industry-wide initiatives and standards.

You will work extremely hard. Look at these pro's and con's from Glassdoor:

Top Review Highlights by Sentiment

Excerpts from user reviews, not authored by Glassdoor

Pros

"You get the chance to work with **great people** that are very driven and know their subject area very well" (in 5552 reviews)

"Work **culture is good** and the flexibility is also great as there are no strict timings to follow." (in 3935 reviews)

"The **benefits are good** they have good work ethics and they take care of their employee's" (in 3657 reviews)

"**Work culture is good** and the flexibility is also great as there are no strict timings to follow." (in 3010 reviews)

"Work with some **great colleagues** and meet lots of intellectual people who are willing to help" (in 1912 reviews)

Cons

"**No work/life balance** and not easy to grow if you are not willing to work crazy hours" (in 9764 reviews)

"**Long hours** are many times overseen (Smart talkers are well recognized than hard workers)" (in 4327 reviews)

"**Low salary** and hard to excel against your peers due to locked in the promotion ladder" (in 3257 reviews)

"**Late working hours** and pressure" (in 2975 reviews)

"The biggest con like working at any other Big 4 firm is the number of hours and the **low pay**." (in 2411 reviews)

Culture and values: The reality

But working at these companies can sometimes feel like two different worlds. Even though they want to work well together and do the right thing, they also have to focus on making money, getting more clients, and staying ahead of competition. This means sometimes they have to make tough choices to reach their goals. These tough choices often play out in how they treat their people. Each of the big 4 has its own variant on off looking after its people, for example

Deloitte has:

Take care of each other
We look out for one another and prioritize respect, fairness, development, and well-being.

PWC has:

Care
- Make the effort to understand every individual and what matters to them
- Recognise the value that each person contributes
- Support others to grow and work in the ways that bring out their best

Reread these statements, but as a partner at the firm. These are not aspirational statements, but harsh economic realities of the position you find yourself.

The reality is that to succeed, you need to keep in mind that you are really just a number on a spreadsheet (*regardless of what anyone says, this is true*) that measures your financial impact, either through billable hours or sales. Outside those parameters, your value diminishes and the treatment you receive will generally worsen. I have come across a few managers that live these values, but I have been witness to many conversations where managers have made it clear that their interest in the wellbeing of an employee extends to their ability to deliver on a project. In addition, your bonuses and promotions are dependent on your ability to make money for the partners, there is no other reason why you will be hired or compensated more. Expect an extremely uncomfortable experience if your billable hours are below target.

In the big 4, and especially the firm where I have been a Senior Director, you need to be the CEO of your own career. No-one cares about you or your career more than you do for yourself.

The Hiring Process

Demand: The recruitment process begins with the identification of a need for a new employee. This could be due to a variety of reasons, such as expansion of the business, replacement of an existing employee, or the need for a specific skill set.

In the Consulting Businesses, the demand for new employees is typically identified by the market offering and the various Go-To-Market leads. This process kicks off once the green light has been given that hiring can take commence. Hiring freezes may be in place due to a weak pipeline, or expected economic weakness and these hiring freezes can continue for a significant amount of time. Demand is validated against the future pipeline of customers and expected utilisation across all the grades. For each potential customer, a list of required roles that must be filled is used to validate the demand with 'bench' resources taking preference.

> EVEN IF THERE IS A SKILLS MISMATCH BETWEEN A BENCH RESOURCE AND A ROLE, BENCH RESOURCES WILL BE USED ANYWAY. THE TERM USED IS PLAYING OUTSIDE YOUR FIELD AND PROVIDE PEOPLE WITH THE OPPORTUNITY TO GROW IN OTHER DISCIPLINES. IT CAN ALSO BE QUITE STRESSFUL, AS YOU MAY BE PLACED IN A ROLE THAT YOU HAVE NO EXPERIENCE OR TRAINING IN, WITH VERY LITTLE SUPPORT FROM YOUR TEAM. I HAVE SEEN ACAREERS TAKE OFF OR BE DESTROYED THROUGH THESE PLACEMENTS. YOU WILL NEED TO BE FLEXIBLE AND PUT IN THE ADDITIONAL HOURS TO LEARN THE NEW TECHNOLOGY AND ENVIRONMENT YOU WILL OPERATE IN AND ALSO HAVE THE ABILITY TO QUICKLY CONNECT WITH THE NEW TEAM AND BUILD A NETWORK FOR SUPPORT.

There is immense pressure on the GTMs and MO leads to reach utilisation and billing targets, with the lower grades expected to have a utilisation of 75% and higher. As a sidenote, it is important that during the interview process, you can focus on how you will remain billable, and more on this when we discuss how to be successful in the interview. The MO and GTM leads will work together to determine the specific requirements for the role, such as the necessary skills, experience, and qualifications.

Job Posting: Once the need for a new employee has been identified, a job posting is created and advertised on various job boards, social media platforms, and the Deloitte website. The job posting typically includes a job description, required qualifications, and instructions on how to apply. The job posting is designed to attract potential candidates who meet the requirements for the role.

Screening: After receiving applications, the recruitment team screens them to identify the most suitable candidates. This may involve reviewing resumes, cover letters, and conducting initial phone or video interviews. The screening process is designed to identify candidates who meet the basic requirements for the role and have the necessary skills and experience. The recruitment team will typically use a set of criteria to evaluate each candidate and determine whether they should move on to the next stage of the process.

Assessment: The next step is to assess the shortlisted candidates through various methods such as online tests, case studies, group discussions, and in-person interviews. The assessment process may vary depending on the role and level of the position. For example, a candidate for a consulting role may be asked to complete a case study, while a candidate for an accounting role may be asked to complete an online test. The assessment process is designed to evaluate the candidate's skills, experience, and fit for the role and the company culture.

Offer: Once the assessment process is complete, the recruitment team makes an offer to the selected candidate. The offer typically includes details such as salary, benefits, start date, and other relevant information. The offer is typically made by the hiring manager or the HR team and is designed to be competitive and attractive to the candidate. The candidate may negotiate the terms of the offer, and the recruitment team will work with them to reach an agreement.

Chapter 2: Preparing Your Application

Tailoring Your CV for the Big 4

Customize Your CV for Each Firm: In the competitive landscape of job applications, particularly when aiming for positions at prestigious Big 4 firms such as Deloitte, PwC, KPMG, and EY, the customization of your CV for each firm becomes not just a recommended step, but a critical component of your application strategy. These firms, known for their distinct cultures, values, and industry focuses, demand more than just a generic resume. By customizing your CV, you communicate not only your awareness of what each firm stands for but also your genuine interest in becoming part of their unique ecosystem. This customization goes beyond merely listing relevant experiences and skills; it involves a deep dive into understanding and aligning with the ethos of each firm, thereby making a compelling case for your candidacy.

> EY: EY HAS ADOPTED A POLICY WHERE NO APPLICATIONS ARE SCREENED OUT BASED SOLELY ON A-LEVEL OR DEGREE GRADES, FOCUSING INSTEAD ON THE SCORES OBTAINED DURING ONLINE ASSESSMENTS.
>
> PWC: PWC REMOVED ITS 2:1 DEGREE CLASSIFICATION REQUIREMENT FOR ALL UNDERGRADUATE AND GRADUATE ROLES, INTERNSHIPS, AND PLACEMENTS TO ATTRACT A MORE DIVERSE APPLICANT POOL.
>
> KPMG: KPMG STATES THAT EVEN IF APPLICANTS DON'T MEET THEIR MINIMUM REQUIREMENTS, THEY WON'T BE AUTOMATICALLY REJECTED, AS THE FIRM ASSESSES SKILLS, STRENGTHS, AND ACHIEVEMENTS AGAINST THEIR GLOBAL BEHAVIOURAL CAPABILITIES

The importance of aligning with a firm's values cannot be overstated. The Big 4 firms are not just looking for candidates with impressive backgrounds; they prioritize individuals whose personal and professional ethos resonates with their own. Tailoring your CV to reflect this alignment does more than tick a box; it demonstrates a thoughtful consideration of where you see yourself fitting within the firm's culture and future. This level of personalization shows that you are not merely looking for any job but are interested in a meaningful career within their specific organization.

Moreover, the relevance of your CV content plays a significant role in capturing the attention of hiring managers. In a sea of applications, a generic CV is likely to be overlooked. Customizing your resume to highlight the skills and experiences that are most pertinent to the position and the firm's current needs ensures that your application speaks directly to what the hiring managers are seeking. This relevance is crucial in demonstrating your potential to contribute from day one, making your application more compelling.

Attention to detail is another critical aspect that is highlighted through a customized CV. The effort you put into tailoring your application does not go unnoticed. It signals to the employer your dedication and professionalism, showing that you are someone who takes their career aspirations seriously. This kind of diligence is highly valued in the professional services industry, where attention to detail and commitment to quality are paramount.

Lastly, in a highly competitive job market, a customized CV provides a competitive edge. It allows you to stand out from the crowd by showcasing not only your qualifications but also your proactive approach and deep understanding of the firm you are applying to. This personalized touch can make all the difference in securing an interview and ultimately, the job. In essence, customizing your CV for each firm you apply to is not just a best practice; it is a strategic move that can significantly elevate your chances of success in the rigorous selection process of the Big 4 firms.

10 steps to customise your CV:

Research Each Big 4 Firm

Why? Understand their unique culture, values, and industry focus.

How? Explore their websites, annual reports, and press releases. Look for clues about what they prioritize.

BIG 4 FIRMS VALUE A BLEND OF TECHNICAL KNOWLEDGE AND SOFT SKILLS, WITH AN EMPHASIS ON PROFESSIONAL QUALIFICATIONS AND RELEVANT EXPERIENCE. CANDIDATES SHOULD HIGHLIGHT THEIR PROFICIENCY IN ACCOUNTING PRINCIPLES AND REGULATIONS, AS WELL AS THEIR ABILITY TO ADAPT TO DIFFERENT ACCOUNTING SOFTWARE AND SYSTEMS.

MOREOVER, THE BIG FOUR SEEK INDIVIDUALS WHO CAN DEMONSTRATE STRONG ANALYTICAL AND PROBLEM-SOLVING SKILLS. THEY APPRECIATE CANDIDATES WHO CAN ANALYZE COMPLEX FINANCIAL DATA TO DERIVE MEANINGFUL INSIGHTS AND SOLUTIONS. COMMUNICATION SKILLS ARE ALSO PARAMOUNT, AS EMPLOYEES MUST EFFECTIVELY CONVEY COMPLEX INFORMATION TO CLIENTS AND TEAM MEMBERS ALIKE.

LEADERSHIP POTENTIAL IS ANOTHER KEY ATTRIBUTE THAT THESE FIRMS CONSIDER. SHOWCASING ANY EXPERIENCE IN LEADING PROJECTS OR TEAMS CAN SET A CANDIDATE APART. ADDITIONALLY, THE ABILITY TO WORK COLLABORATIVELY WITHIN DIVERSE TEAMS IS HIGHLY REGARDED, AS IT REFLECTS THE GLOBAL AND INCLUSIVE NATURE OF THESE ORGANIZATIONS.

LASTLY, PERSONAL ACHIEVEMENTS AND EXTRACURRICULAR ACTIVITIES THAT EXHIBIT A CANDIDATE'S DRIVE, AMBITION, AND WELL-ROUNDED CHARACTER CAN BE INFLUENTIAL. IT'S ABOUT STRIKING A BALANCE BETWEEN PROFESSIONAL COMPETENCIES AND PERSONAL QUALITIES THAT ALIGN WITH THE FIRM'S VALUES AND CULTURE.

Before tailoring your CV, thoroughly research the specific Big 4 firm in London you're applying to (Deloitte, PwC, KPMG, EY). Identify their core values, industry focuses, and any recent projects or initiatives they have undertaken. For example, if EY is emphasizing sustainability and you've worked on a sustainability project during your university years in India, make sure to highlight this experience prominently in your CV.

Customize Your Professional Summary

Why? Your professional summary and objective sets the tone. Make it relevant.

Start your CV with a brief professional summary that articulates your career aspirations and how they align with the firm's goals. For instance, if applying to KPMG London, and you're passionate about financial auditing, mention your aspiration to contribute to their auditing team, drawing on your robust academic background in finance from India and any relevant internships.

The Aspiring Auditor with International Flair Rajiv was determined to join KPMG's London office, drawn by their reputation in financial auditing. With a solid academic background in finance from one of India's top universities and an internship at a reputable audit firm in Mumbai, Rajiv tailored his professional summary to highlight his aspiration to contribute to KPMG's auditing team. He emphasized his understanding of diverse accounting practices and his eagerness to apply his international experience to the complex, global client base that KPMG serves. This customized approach demonstrated Rajiv's alignment with KPMG's global outlook and his specific interest in auditing, making his application stand out.

The Tech-Savvy Consultant Anita, aiming for a position at Deloitte's consulting division, knew that showcasing her tech expertise would be crucial. Having developed a solid foundation in digital transformation strategies during her MBA, coupled with hands-on experience in a tech startup, she crafted her professional summary to reflect her passion for leveraging technology to solve business challenges. Anita specifically mentioned her desire to join Deloitte's team to contribute to their digital initiatives, highlighting her unique blend of business acumen and tech-savviness. Her tailored summary immediately caught the attention of recruiters looking for candidates with a strong consulting background and a keen interest in technology.

The Sustainability Champion Liam, with a master's degree in Environmental Management and experience working on sustainability projects, was keen on joining EY's sustainability consulting practice. In his professional summary, Liam articulated his commitment to promoting sustainable business practices and his ambition to support EY's mission to drive sustainability transformations for their clients. He outlined his experience in conducting environmental impact assessments and implementing sustainability initiatives, positioning himself as an ideal candidate for EY's forward-thinking sustainability agenda. This customization ensured that his application resonated with EY's values and strategic goals.

The Financial Strategist Eyeing PwC Sophia targeted PwC's financial consulting team, recognizing her strength in financial strategy and analysis. Her background included a finance degree from a prestigious university and experience in a financial strategy role within the finance industry. In her professional summary, Sophia expressed her aspiration to apply her analytical skills and strategic thinking to help PwC's clients navigate their financial challenges. She mentioned her keen interest in joining PwC's renowned financial consulting team to contribute to and learn from the best in the industry. This targeted approach made her application compelling to PwC recruiters seeking candidates with a solid foundation in finance and a clear career direction.

Highlight Relevant Experience

Why? Big 4 firms value practical experience.

Match your academic projects, internships, and any part-time work experiences with the skills and expertise the firm is looking for. Suppose you interned with a financial consultancy in India; detail your role, the skills you developed, and how they are relevant to the services provided by the Big 4 firm you're applying to, particularly those that are valued in the London market.

Big 4 firms also value diversity and global perspectives. If you've participated in international conferences, student exchange programs, or have been part of global virtual teams during your studies, include these experiences to showcase your ability to adapt and work in multicultural environments.

Quantify Achievements

Why? Numbers grab attention.

Where possible, use numbers to quantify your achievements in previous roles or projects.

The Efficiency Innovator Vikram, an engineering graduate from India, led a university project focused on optimizing manufacturing processes. By introducing a lean manufacturing technique, his team was able to reduce waste and increase efficiency by 15%. When applying to Deloitte's operations consulting division, Vikram highlighted this achievement in his CV, specifying the percentage improvement and briefly describing the methods used. During his interview, he elaborated on how this experience equipped him with a keen eye for identifying and implementing process improvements. This quantified achievement not only showcased his leadership but also his ability to make a significant, measurable impact, aligning with the results-driven culture at Deloitte.

The Revenue Booster Sophia, with a background in digital marketing, worked for a startup where her campaign strategies led to a 30% increase in online sales over six months. As she aimed to transition into consulting with a focus on digital transformation at KPMG London, she made sure to quantify this achievement in her application. By detailing the strategy and execution that led to the revenue boost, Sophia demonstrated her direct contribution to business growth. This clear evidence of her ability to drive tangible business outcomes was instrumental in advancing her candidacy during the recruitment process.

The Cost-Cutting Analyst After completing his MBA, Aarav worked for a mid-sized firm where he was part of a project team that reduced operational costs by 20% through strategic supplier negotiations and inventory management improvements. Aiming to leverage his experience in financial consulting at EY, Aarav included this achievement in his resume, highlighting the specific percentage reduction in costs and the strategies employed to achieve it. During his interview, Aarav discussed the analytical and negotiation skills he honed during the project, underscoring his capacity to contribute to cost-efficiency goals at EY.

The Client Satisfaction Leader Lena, a customer service manager, implemented new training programs and a feedback system that led to a 25% improvement in customer satisfaction ratings within a year. As she sought a career in management consulting at PwC, focusing on customer experience improvement, Lena quantified this achievement in her application. She detailed the steps taken to achieve this increase and how it positively impacted the company's reputation and client retention rates. This quantifiable success not only highlighted her leadership and strategic thinking skills but also aligned with PwC's emphasis on delivering exceptional client service.

Emphasize Transferable Skills

Why? Consulting requires diverse skills.

Example: "Strong problem-solving skills from coursework and teamwork projects."

Include Relevant Certifications

Why? Big 4 firms value qualifications.

If you have pursued professional certifications relevant to the accounting and finance industry, such as Chartered Accountant (CA) from India, mention these. Also, include extracurricular activities that demonstrate skills relevant to consulting and business services, such as leadership roles in student societies or volunteer work with NGOs.

Tailor Your Education Section

Why? Highlight relevant courses.

While your degree may be well-recognized in India, it's important to provide context for UK employers. Include any equivalent UK qualifications or GPA conversions, and highlight coursework relevant to the job you're applying for. For example, if you've taken advanced courses in audit and assurance, make sure this is clear in your education section. For instance, the UK National Academic Recognition Information Centre (UK NARIC) provides a table comparing overseas qualifications to British degree standards.

Personalize Your Interests Section

Why? Show your personality.

Example: "Passionate about data analytics, cricket, and volunteering."

Use Keywords from Job Descriptions

Why? ATS systems scan for relevant terms.

Analyse the job listing carefully and incorporate keywords and phrases into your CV. This not only helps in passing the Applicant Tracking Systems (ATS) but also shows that you have a keen eye for detail. For example, if "analytical skills" and "team collaboration" are frequently mentioned, ensure these are reflected in your descriptions of past roles and projects.

Seek Feedback from Peers and Mentors

Why? Fresh eyes catch nuances.

Ensure your CV is free from errors and clearly communicates your suitability for the role. It can be beneficial to have a mentor or professional from the industry, possibly through LinkedIn connections or alumni networks, review your CV. Their insights can provide valuable feedback and help you further tailor your application.

Crafting a standout cover letter

Why Is a Cover Letter Important? A cover letter is your personal advocate, going beyond the bullet points of your resume to tell the story behind your professional journey. A resume might stay constant, but a cover letter is your chance to speak directly to the needs and culture of the Big 4 firm you are targeting. This personal touch can make a world of difference. Use the cover letter to draw clear connections between your accomplishments and the qualities the firm values. Whether it's your knack for solving complex problems or your commitment to ethical financial practices, show them why you're a perfect match. In a pool of similarly qualified candidates, your cover letter is an opportunity to stand out. Maybe it's your experience with non-profit organizations in India that demonstrates your leadership and commitment to community, or perhaps it's a unique project that showcases your innovative approach to traditional problems.

What Recruiters and Hiring Managers Look for in a Cover Letter

Recruiters and hiring managers are inundated with applications. To capture their attention, your cover letter must have:

TIPS AND TRICKS FOR AN OUTSTANDING COVER LETTER:

AN OUTSTANDING COVER LETTER CAN SIGNIFICANTLY BOOST YOUR CHANCES OF LANDING AN INTERVIEW. HERE'S HOW TO MAKE YOURS STAND OUT:

HOOK THEM EARLY: BEGIN WITH SOMETHING MEMORABLE. THIS COULD BE A BRIEF STORY ABOUT A PROFESSIONAL ACCOMPLISHMENT, A PERSONAL PROJECT, OR A MOMENT THAT DEFINES YOUR CAREER PATH.

ADDRESS PAIN POINTS: DO SOME RESEARCH TO UNDERSTAND THE CHALLENGES THE COMPANY OR INDUSTRY IS FACING AND SUGGEST HOW YOU COULD HELP ADDRESS THEM. THIS SHOWS FORESIGHT AND INITIATIVE.

USE KEYWORDS: SCAN THE JOB DESCRIPTION FOR SPECIFIC SKILLS AND QUALIFICATIONS THEY'RE SEEKING AND WEAVE THESE KEYWORDS INTO YOUR LETTER NATURALLY.

Clarity and Conciseness They value cover letters that get to the point quickly while clearly articulating how you can add value to their team.

Customization A cover letter that addresses the hiring manager by name and mentions specific aspects of the job listing shows that you've done your homework and are genuinely interested in the role.

Relevance Connecting your past achievements to the job you're applying for demonstrates that you understand what's required and that you have what it takes to excel.

Passion and Enthusiasm A recruiter can tell when a candidate is excited about the opportunity. Let your genuine interest in both the role and the company's mission shine through.

Attention to Detail A single typo can undermine your application. Demonstrating attention to detail by proofreading your cover letter reflects on your professionalism and diligence.

Storytelling Illustrate your qualifications with real-world examples. Stories of overcoming challenges or making significant contributions at your previous positions are much more compelling than lists of duties.

Alignment with Company Values Big 4 firms pride themselves on their culture and values. Highlight how your personal and professional values align with theirs, be it through commitment to excellence, integrity, or community service.

What to avoid in cover letters

Generic Openings Tailor your introduction to the role and company, showing that you've made an effort to understand who they are.

Repeating Your Resume Your cover letter should offer new insights and details about your experiences and how they make you a great fit for the position.

Negativity Always maintain a positive tone, even when discussing challenges or difficult situations from past roles.

Overused Phrases Avoid buzzwords that don't add value or substance to your application.

Lengthy Paragraphs Keep your sentences and paragraphs short and to the point to maintain the reader's interest.

Sample Cover Letter

Dear [Hiring Manager's Name],

I am excited to express my interest in the SAP Basis Consultant position at [Company Name], as advertised on [where you found the job posting]. With over 10 years of dedicated experience in the SAP Basis domain, particularly with SAP ECC and SAP BW, I am eager to bring my expertise to your innovative team, contributing to [Company's Name]'s commitment to [something you admire about the company, aligning with their mission or a recent achievement].

During my tenure at [Previous Company Name], I spearheaded a critical upgrade project for SAP ECC, leading to a 30% improvement in system performance and a significant reduction in downtime. This experience honed my skills in Basis Administration, particularly in Transports and Change Management, allowing me to ensure seamless, efficient operations and enhance system reliability across departments.

One project I'm particularly proud of involved optimizing the performance of SAP HANA for a client facing frequent outages. By implementing targeted changes and conducting thorough training sessions for the in-house team, we achieved a 99.9% system uptime, enhancing productivity and stakeholder satisfaction.

I am passionate about leveraging my expertise in system security, monitoring, and incident management to address and pre-empt challenges. My approach to troubleshooting SAP application issues is not just technical but also strategic, focusing on preventive measures and user training to minimize future disruptions.

Joining [Company Name] excites me because of your dedication to [mention any known company initiatives related to SAP or technology innovations], and I am keen to contribute to such a forward-thinking environment. I am particularly impressed by [something specific about the company or its culture], which aligns with my professional values and approach to SAP consultancy.

Thank you for considering my application. I am looking forward to the opportunity to discuss how my background, skills, and enthusiasms can contribute to the continued success and growth of [Company Name]. I am eager to learn more about your team's goals and how I can assist in reaching them.

Warm regards,

[Your Name]

Essential Qualifications and Certifications

Securing a position at one of the Big 4 firms in London requires not just a wealth of experience but also a solid foundation of relevant qualifications and certifications. These credentials not only demonstrate your commitment to your profession but also your readiness to meet the high standards of these globally recognized companies.

> EARLY IN MY CAREER, ONE OF THE DIRECTORS I WORKED FOR, WHO LED OUR DIVISION, HAD NO DEGREE OR FORMAL SAP CERTIFICATIONS. HOWEVER, THIS DIRECTOR POSSESSED PASSION AND DRIVE TO CONTINUALLY LEARN AND STAY AT THE CUTTING EDGE OF NEW TECHNOLOGY. ADDITIONALLY, HE DILIGENTLY CULTIVATED RELATIONSHIPS WITH SAP AND BECAME THE GO-TO PERSON FOR ANYTHING RELATED TO SAP'S NEW TECHNOLOGY. THIS DEMONSTRATES THAT FORMAL EDUCATION IS NOT SUFFICIENT; DRIVE, PASSION, AND CONTINUOUS LEARNING PLAY SIGNIFICANT ROLES IN BEING HIRED, RECOGNIZED, AND REWARDED.

> AS A HIRING MANAGER, FORMAL EDUCATION PLAYED A LESSER ROLE WHEN FILLING EXPERIENCED POSITIONS SUCH AS SENIOR CONSULTANT AND ABOVE. I TENDED TO ASSESS HOW CANDIDATES SUPPLEMENTED THEIR QUALIFICATIONS WITH EXPERIENCE AND HOW THEY APPLIED THEIR KNOWLEDGE TO SOLVE REAL-WORLD PROBLEMS FOR CUSTOMERS. IN FACT, IN MOST CASES, HAVING A BACHELOR'S OR MASTER'S DEGREE WAS SIMPLY A MENTAL CHECKMARK I MADE DURING INTERVIEWS. EXPERIENCE HAS TAUGHT ME THAT DEGREES ALONE DO NOT GUARANTEE SUCCESS AS INDIVIDUALS PROGRESS IN THEIR CAREERS.

Here's a breakdown of the essential qualifications and certifications that can significantly enhance your candidacy:

Academic Qualifications

Bachelor's Degree A bachelor's degree in fields such as Business, Accounting, Finance, Information Technology, or related areas is typically the minimum requirement. For positions that are more specialized, such as consulting or advisory roles, a degree relevant to the specialization is preferred.

Master's Degree or MBA Though not always mandatory, a master's degree or an MBA can be a significant advantage, especially for management-level positions or roles requiring specialized knowledge.

Professional Certifications

Chartered Accountant (CA) or Certified Public Accountant (CPA) For roles in audit, tax, and accounting, being a qualified CA or CPA is often essential. These certifications are proof of your expertise in accounting principles and practices.

Certified Information Systems Auditor (CISA) For roles in IT audit or cybersecurity, a CISA certification can demonstrate your ability to audit, control, and provide assurance of information systems.

Certified Information Security Manager (CISM) If you're targeting positions in information security management, a CISM certification can show your understanding of governance, risk management, and information security program development and management.

Project Management Professional (PMP) For project management roles, a PMP certification from the Project Management Institute (PMI) can be crucial. It showcases your competence in leading and directing projects and teams.

Chartered Financial Analyst (CFA) For roles in finance, investment management, or advisory services, a CFA charter can provide an edge, indicating a strong foundation in advanced investment analysis and real-world portfolio management skills.

Additional Credentials and Skills:

Language Proficiency For the global and multicultural environment of the Big 4 in London, proficiency in multiple languages can be an advantage, particularly in client-facing roles.

Technology Certifications Depending on your field, certifications in specific software, platforms, or technologies relevant to your role (e.g., SAP Certified Professional, Microsoft Certified: Azure Solutions Architect Expert, etc.) can set you apart from other candidates.

Soft Skills While not formal qualifications, soft skills such as leadership, communication, analytical thinking, and problem-solving are crucial. Evidence of these skills, through leadership roles, team projects, or other activities, can complement your academic and professional credentials.

HARD SKILLS MAY SECURE YOU THE INTERVIEW, BUT IT'S THE SOFT SKILLS THAT CLINCH THE JOB. CAN YOU COMMUNICATE CLEARLY, CONCISELY, AND ADDRESS THE POINT? NOTHING'S WORSE THAN AN HOUR-LONG INTERVIEW WHERE MY QUESTIONS REMAIN UNANSWERED.

Continuous Learning

Commitment to Continuous Professional Development The Big 4 firms value candidates who demonstrate a commitment to learning and adapting to new skills and knowledge. Participation in workshops, seminars, and courses related to your field can show your dedication to staying at the forefront of your profession.

Building a professional online presence

In the digital era, your online presence can be as critical as your resume. For aspiring professionals looking to land a job at a Big Four firm in the UK, a polished and professional online persona is essential. Here's how you can build an online presence that stands out.

Audit Your Online Presence Start by Googling yourself to see what potential employers might find. Ensure that all public information presents you in a professional light. Remove or privatize any content that doesn't align with the professional image you want to portray.

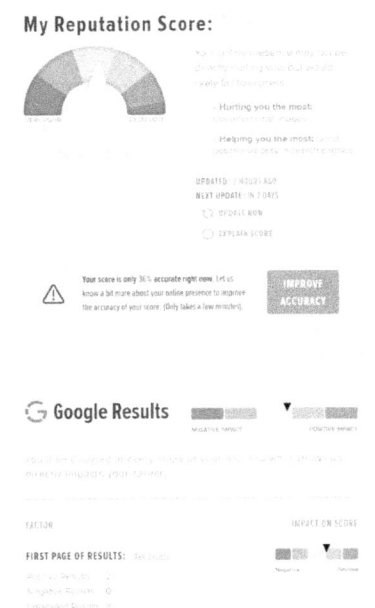

Beyond Google, consider using tools like BrandYourself, which can help identify and improve any digital footprint aspects that might not reflect well on you professionally. This could include old blog posts, forgotten social media accounts, or any online mentions that don't align with your professional goals.

There have been numerous cases where individuals lost job offers or were fired due to inappropriate or offensive content discovered online. For example, a candidate might lose an offer from a Big Four firm if their social media profiles contain derogatory comments or content that conflicts with the firm's values of inclusivity and professionalism. There is a famous incident in 2020, where a Deloitte Harvard grad, Claira Janover, lost her job over a poorly judged TikTok video.

Optimize Your LinkedIn Profile LinkedIn is the go-to platform for professional networking. Make sure your profile is complete with a professional photo, a compelling headline, and a detailed summary of your skills and experience.

Regularly update your profile with new achievements and engage with content relevant to your field.

Your profile photo is the first visual cue that speaks to your professionalism. Choose a high-quality, recent headshot that aligns with the industry standards of the Big Four firms. A professional photo conveys trustworthiness and approachability.

A bad LinkedIn profile photo can negatively impact your professional image. Here are some common mistakes to avoid:

No Photo: A missing profile picture can make your profile seem incomplete or neglected.

Inappropriate Attire: Dressing in a casual or unprofessional manner can undermine your credibility.

Poor Quality: Blurry, poorly lit, or low-resolution photos can give an impression of unprofessionalism.

Distracting Backgrounds: Busy or cluttered backgrounds can take the focus away from you.

Non-Professional Expression: Overly casual or inappropriate facial expressions can detract from the professional appeal.

Group Shots: Photos that include other people can be confusing as to who the profile belongs to.

Cropped Images: Pictures where it's obvious someone else has been cropped out can appear unprofessional.

Logos or Graphics: Using a company logo or unrelated graphic instead of a personal photo is not recommended.

Compelling Headline Your headline should succinctly encapsulate your professional identity, expertise, and aspirations. Use keywords that are relevant to your desired role and industry to improve your visibility in searches by recruiters.

Detailed Summary The summary section is your opportunity to tell your story. Highlight your unique skills, experiences, and career goals. Use a narrative style to engage readers and make your profile memorable.

Regular Updates Keep your profile current by regularly adding new achievements, certifications, or skills. This demonstrates your commitment to professional growth and keeps your network informed of your progress.

Engage with Industry-Relevant Content Active participation in online forums and industry groups can lead to valuable networking opportunities. Share your insights, ask questions, and contribute to discussions to increase your visibility and establish yourself as a knowledgeable professional in your field.

Create a Personal Website or Portfolio If applicable, a personal website or portfolio can showcase your work, achievements, and skills. Use platforms like

WordPress or Squarespace to create a professional site that you *can* share with recruiters.

Consistency Across Platforms Ensure that your online presence is consistent across different platforms. Use the same professional photo and similar language to describe your skills and experiences, whether on LinkedIn, Twitter, or your personal website.

Monitor and Update Regularly Your online presence is an evolving reflection of your professional life. Regularly update your profiles to reflect your current position, skills, and accomplishments. This shows potential employers that you are active and engaged in your career development.

Chapter 3: Networking

In the early stages of my career, I've navigated through a complex relationship with the concept of networking. Initially, during my college days, networking struck me as overly transactional—an exercise in cultivating relationships primarily for self-advancement. The mere thought of engaging in superficial chit-chat with strangers not only heightened my social anxiety but also seemed to contradict my values around authenticity and genuine connection. This perspective, however, has significantly evolved as I've matured professionally.

> WHEN ERIC PALMER STEPPED INTO HIS NEW ROLE AS DIRECTOR IN CONSULTING, EXPANDING HIS NETWORK WAS THE FURTHEST THING FROM HIS MIND. HIS MAIN CHALLENGE? TIME. HOW COULD HE FIND THE HOURS TO LEAD HIS TEAM THROUGH A MAJOR TRANSFORMATION PROJECT AND STILL THINK ABOUT STRATEGIC MATTERS LIKE BUSINESS EXPANSION? HIS SOLUTION: LOCKING HIMSELF—LITERALLY—IN HIS OFFICE TO CARVE OUT TIME AND STILL MAKE IT HOME TO HIS FAMILY AT A DECENT HOUR. YET, AMIDST THE DAY-TO-DAY ISSUES LIKE RECURRING CONFLICTS WITHIN HIS TEAM, NETWORKING SEEMED LIKE A LUXURY HE COULDN'T AFFORD. BUT WHEN A NEW CUSTOMER WAS ACQUIRED AND PRESENTED AT A LEADERSHIP MEETING WITHOUT HIS INPUT, HE ABRUPTLY REALIZED HE WAS OUT OF THE LOOP—NOT JUST WITHIN THE FIRM, BUT OUTSIDE TOO—AT A CRUCIAL MOMENT FOR HIS FUTURE IN THE COMPANY.
>
> ERIC'S SITUATION ISN'T UNIQUE. OVER THE PAST TWO YEARS, WE'VE BEEN TRACKING A COHORT OF 30 MANAGERS NAVIGATING WHAT WE TERM THE LEADERSHIP TRANSITION—A PIVOTAL POINT IN THEIR CAREERS THAT DEMANDS THEY RECONSIDER BOTH THEMSELVES AND THEIR ROLES. THROUGH THIS PROCESS, WE'VE DISCOVERED THAT NETWORKING—BUILDING A NETWORK OF PERSONAL CONTACTS WHO PROVIDE SUPPORT, FEEDBACK, INSIGHT, RESOURCES, AND INFORMATION—IS BOTH ONE OF THE MOST OBVIOUS AND ONE OF THE MOST DREADED DEVELOPMENTAL CHALLENGES ASPIRING LEADERS MUST CONFRONT.

I've come to understand that networking is far from merely a tool for opportunistic career advancement. Indeed, while it's undeniable that networking plays a pivotal role in job acquisition and unlocking new professional avenues, its essence lies in forging sincere relationships, sharing knowledge, and contributing positively to the lives of others. The approach one takes toward networking can transform it from a self-serving activity into a mutually beneficial exchange of ideas, support, and resources.

For those who find themselves wrestling with misconceptions about networking, feeling anxious about engaging with it, or simply uncertain about its value and how to begin, there is ample guidance available. Drawing from a wealth of advice from seasoned professionals, it's possible to navigate the networking landscape in a manner that aligns with your personal ethics and comfort level.

The significance of networking cannot be overstated, particularly in the context of professional development and career trajectory. Empirical evidence consistently highlights the correlation between a robust professional network and career success indicators such as higher salaries, more frequent promotions, and greater job satisfaction. This correlation is intuitive; being well-connected across various levels and sectors increases your visibility to potential opportunities and key decision-makers. For example, having a senior colleague who is aware of your contributions and achievements can significantly boost your chances of being recommended for upward mobility within your organization. Similarly, a connection within another company can be instrumental in ensuring your resume lands in the hands of a hiring manager when a suitable vacancy arises.

Moreover, networking serves as a dynamic platform for continuous learning and personal growth. Engaging with a diverse array of individuals allows for the exchange of valuable feedback, industry insights, and organizational culture tips. Whether seeking advice from peers on a project, extracting industry trends from a thought leader on LinkedIn, or understanding the nuances of your organization's culture through a conversation with a senior team member, these interactions can substantially enhance your knowledge base, skill set, and overall performance.

Most individuals lean towards a primary motivational outlook when it comes to networking, typically classified by psychologists as either a "promotion" mindset or a "prevention" mindset. Individuals with a promotion mindset view networking through the lens of potential gains—focusing on the opportunities for growth, progress, and achievements it can provide. Conversely, those with a prevention mindset perceive networking as a professional obligation, a task they must undertake despite personal feelings.

Through a series of experiments conducted in the United States and Italy involving college students, working adults, and a specific study of 174 lawyers at a law firm, we observed the impact of these distinct mental approaches. Individuals driven by a promotion-focused mentality engaged in networking with enthusiasm, fuelled by a sense of curiosity and openness to the myriad possibilities that could emerge. On the other hand, individuals with a prevention-focused outlook viewed networking as an unwelcome necessity, often feeling disingenuous during these interactions. Consequently, they engaged in networking less frequently, which negatively affected certain job performance metrics. However, research by Carol Dweck of Stanford University highlights that shifting one's mindset from prevention to promotion is possible, thereby transforming networking from a perceived burden into an exciting chance for exploration and learning.

Consider your reaction to a mandatory work-related social event. You might think, "I dislike these types of gatherings. I'll have to feign enjoyment and mingle unwillingly." Alternatively, you could adopt a more positive outlook: "This could turn out to be interesting. Unexpectedly, it might lead to a conversation that sparks new ideas and opens doors to new experiences and opportunities."

While introverts cannot simply become extroverts, choosing your motivational focus in networking situations is within everyone's grasp. By focusing on the benefits—how networking can enhance your knowledge and skills relevant to your job—the activity can start to feel more engaging and valuable.

In essence, effective networking transcends the simplistic view of it as a means to an end. When approached with intentionality and a spirit of reciprocity, it can foster profound personal and professional development, enriching not only your career path but also contributing to a broader culture of collaboration and growth.

Networking Strategies

In the landscape of professional development, networking emerges as a cornerstone, essential for broadening horizons and opening doors to uncharted career paths. Yet, navigating the networking world requires more than mere participation; it necessitates a strategic approach tailored to fostering authentic and mutually beneficial relationships. This section delves into effective networking strategies that can transform the way you connect with others, ensuring that your networking efforts are both meaningful and impactful.

Embrace a Mindset of Giving

Embracing a mindset of giving transforms networking from a mere transactional endeavour into a rich, fulfilling journey of mutual growth and support. This approach, rooted in generosity and service, underscores the idea that the most meaningful professional relationships are built on the foundation of reciprocal value.

When you enter interactions with the mindset of what you can contribute rather than what you can extract, your connections become more authentic. People are naturally drawn to individuals who show genuine interest in their well-being and success. By offering your expertise or assistance without immediate expectations of return, you lay the groundwork for relationships based on trust and mutual respect, which are more likely to endure and be fruitful over time.

Offering your skills, knowledge, or time to help others positions you as a valuable resource within your network. This could involve sharing your technical knowledge, providing feedback on a project, or offering career advice to someone just starting in your field. When you are known as someone who contributes meaningfully to others' success, your reputation as a supportive and reliable professional grows. This not only elevates your standing within your current network but also encourages others to recommend you to their connections, thereby expanding your network further.

The act of giving—be it through mentoring, advising, or simply sharing knowledge—also serves as an opportunity for you to refine your own skills and deepen your understanding. Teaching or advising others challenges you to articulate your knowledge clearly and may expose you to new perspectives or questions you hadn't considered. This process of giving back can be a powerful tool for your own personal and professional development.

By prioritizing giving within your networking efforts, you contribute to a culture of generosity and reciprocity. This culture encourages others to also share their resources and support, creating a virtuous cycle of giving and receiving within your professional community. In such an environment, everyone benefits, and the collective resources, knowledge, and support available to the network are amplified.

Often, the most transformative opportunities arise from relationships where you least expect them. By consistently offering help and support, you might open doors to collaborations, job offers, partnerships, or mentorships that you hadn't anticipated. These opportunities frequently emerge not as a direct result of seeking them out but as a natura l byproduct of the value you've provided to others.

Lastly, embracing a giving mindset enriches your own professional journey with a sense of fulfilment and purpose. Knowing that you've played a part in someone else's success story adds a layer of meaning to your work that transcends traditional measures of success. This sense of contribution and impact can be deeply satisfying and motivating, driving you to continue growing and giving within your professional community.

Diversify Your Network

Diversifying your network is akin to cultivating a rich, multifaceted garden that thrives on variety. In the ecosystem of professional networking, the inclusion of a broad spectrum of individuals from different industries, backgrounds, and career stages enriches your professional life, bringing in fresh ideas, perspectives, and opportunities that you might not encounter in a more homogenous setting.

Venturing beyond the confines of your current industry or profession exposes you to new trends, technologies, and methodologies that could be transferable or beneficial to your own field. For instance, a tech professional might gain insights into innovative customer engagement strategies from someone in the marketing sector, or a finance expert could learn about risk management techniques from a seasoned entrepreneur. This cross-pollination of ideas not only broadens your knowledge but can also spark innovative solutions to problems in your own domain.

Connecting with individuals from diverse geographical and cultural backgrounds can significantly enhance your global awareness and cultural sensitivity, attributes that are increasingly valuable in today's interconnected world. This global perspective is not just about understanding different cultures but also about appreciating the nuances of conducting business across borders, which can be crucial for career advancement in multinational companies or for entrepreneurs looking to expand their operations internationally.

Exposure to different ways of thinking and problem-solving can stimulate creativity and innovation. When you interact with people who have varied experiences and viewpoints, you're more likely to consider alternative solutions and approaches. This diversity of thought can be especially beneficial in brainstorming sessions or project planning, leading to more creative and effective outcomes.

A diverse network can be invaluable when you're considering a career change or looking to pivot to a new industry. Connections in various fields can provide insights into new sectors, recommend educational resources, or even refer you to open positions in their companies. Their guidance can help demystify the challenges of transitioning between careers and offer practical advice based on their experiences.

A network that includes individuals at different stages of their professional journeys offers a unique support system. Seasoned professionals can provide mentorship, sharing their wisdom and lessons learned throughout their careers. Peers can offer camaraderie and the opportunity to share current challenges and successes. Meanwhile, connecting with those earlier in their career journey can remind you of your own growth and allow you to pay it forward by offering guidance and support.

Finally, a diverse network opens the door to opportunities that you might not have otherwise encountered. These could range from speaking engagements, consulting projects, and collaborative ventures to more personal opportunities like finding a mentor or becoming one. Sometimes, the most groundbreaking opportunities arise from the most unexpected connections.

Leverage Social Media Wisely

Leveraging social media wisely in the realm of professional networking has become an indispensable strategy for modern professionals. Platforms such as

LinkedIn have not only democratized networking by breaking down geographical barriers but have also provided a dynamic arena for professionals to showcase their expertise, achievements, and professional aspirations. To maximize the benefits of social media networking, a strategic and thoughtful approach is crucial.

Your social media profiles serve as your digital business card. Ensure that your LinkedIn profile is comprehensive, up-to-date, and reflects your professional image accurately. This includes a professional photo, a compelling summary that highlights your strengths and achievements, and a detailed account of your work experience and skills. Your online presence should tell your professional story in a way that captivates and engages your intended audience.

Position yourself as a thought leader in your field by regularly sharing insightful articles, posting engaging content, and contributing to discussions relevant to your industry. This could involve writing articles on LinkedIn, sharing industry news with your commentary, or creating content that addresses common challenges in your field. The aim is to provide value to your network, fostering a reputation as a knowledgeable and resourceful professional.

Networking is as much about uplifting others as it is about advancing your own career. Make it a habit to celebrate the achievements of your connections by sharing their accomplishments, endorsing their skills, and writing recommendations. This not only strengthens your relationships but also encourages a culture of mutual support and recognition within your network.

Beyond sharing content, genuine engagement with your connections' posts is vital. This means leaving thoughtful comments, asking questions, and sparking conversations. Such interactions show that you are not just there to broadcast your achievements but are also interested in learning from and engaging with your peers. It demonstrates your willingness to be an active participant in your professional community.

While social media offers a convenient platform for initial introductions, the depth of professional relationships is often cultivated through face-to-face interactions. Whenever possible, take the initiative to move beyond the digital realm. This could mean inviting a connection for a coffee chat, arranging a phone call, or meeting at industry events. These real-world interactions can solidify your professional relationships, transforming them from mere online connections to valuable members of your network.

Many social media platforms host industry-specific groups that allow you to dive deeper into your professional interests, stay abreast of the latest industry trends, and connect with like-minded individuals. Active participation in these groups can further establish your expertise and open up opportunities for collaboration and knowledge sharing.

Remember, the digital footprint you leave on social media is lasting. Always communicate with professionalism and respect, keeping in mind that your interactions are visible to your entire professional network and potentially beyond. This respect for digital etiquette not only reflects well on your personal brand but also fosters a positive and productive online community.

Attend Events with Purpose

While attending networking events, conferences, and workshops is a traditional strategy, doing so with intention can significantly enhance their value. Before stepping into any event, clarity on what you aim to achieve is crucial. Are you looking to gain insights into a new industry trend? Do you wish to meet potential mentors, employers, or collaborators? Or perhaps you're exploring job opportunities within a specific field. By defining your objectives upfront, you set a navigational compass that will guide your actions throughout the event.

Familiarize yourself with the event's agenda, speakers, and attendee list (if available). This research will help you pinpoint which sessions to attend, whom to seek out, and what topics might serve as conversation starters. Many events offer apps or online platforms where attendees can connect and schedule meetings in advance — make use of these tools to maximize your opportunities for meaningful engagement.

Having a succinct and compelling way to introduce yourself is invaluable in a networking context. Your elevator pitch should communicate who you are, what you do, and what makes you unique, all within a brief timeframe. Tailor your pitch to the event and your objectives, ensuring it resonates with the people you're most interested in connecting with. While the temptation to meet as many people as possible can be strong, focusing on the quality of connections rather than quantity often yields better results. Seek out interactions that align with your goals and invest time in conversations that are mutually engaging. Remember, a few meaningful connections can be more valuable than a stack of business cards from brief exchanges.

Be present in your interactions, showing genuine interest in others. Active listening not only demonstrates respect but also helps you gather information and insights that could be crucial for your professional growth. Ask thoughtful questions that encourage deeper conversation and share your own experiences and knowledge where relevant.

After the event, the real work begins. Follow up promptly with new connections, referencing specific details from your conversation to reinforce the connection. Whether it's through LinkedIn, email, or a phone call, reaching out shows that you value the relationship and are interested in keeping the dialogue going. Propose a next step, such as a meeting or a simple exchange of articles or resources, to continue building the relationship. Post-event, take time to reflect on your experiences. What worked well? What could be improved? How can you further engage with the connections you've made? Use these reflections to refine your strategy for future events and to take concrete steps towards integrating new connections into your professional network.

Cultivate Active Listening

Cultivating active listening is a cornerstone of effective networking, transforming superficial exchanges into deep, meaningful connections. This skill goes beyond merely hearing words; it involves engaging fully with the speaker, processing their message, and responding in a way that demonstrates genuine understanding and interest.

Active listening fosters a level of engagement that signals to the speaker your genuine interest in their message. By giving someone your full attention—free from distractions or the urge to plan your next response—you create a space where meaningful exchange can flourish. This genuine engagement helps in breaking down barriers and building trust, essential components of strong professional relationships.

By actively listening, you not only grasp the surface-level content of what's being shared but also the underlying messages, such as the speaker's values, needs, and motivations. This deeper understanding enables you to recall the details of the conversation more accurately, facilitating richer follow-up discussions. It's this level of detail and attentiveness that can distinguish you as a thoughtful and valuable connection in the eyes of others.

Active listening is a powerful tool for building rapport. When people feel heard and understood, they are more likely to open up and share more freely. This exchange deepens the connection and lays a foundation of trust. Acknowledging the speaker's ideas and feelings, whether through verbal affirmations or non-verbal cues like nodding, communicates that you value their perspective, further strengthening the relationship.

In demonstrating active listening, you encourage a culture of openness and collaboration. Conversations become two-way streets where ideas can be exchanged freely and constructively. This environment is ripe for innovation, problem-solving, and mutual support, where all parties feel valued and are more inclined to contribute their best.

Active listening plays a critical role in resolving misunderstandings or conflicts that may arise in professional settings. By listening intently to understand the other party's viewpoint, you're better positioned to address concerns and work towards a resolution. This approach can turn potential conflicts into opportunities for growth and learning.

Practicing active listening develops your empathy and emotional intelligence, key traits for successful networking and leadership. Understanding and resonating with the emotions behind someone's words allows for more compassionate and appropriate responses, fostering a deeper connection and respect between professionals.

Here are some strategies to Cultivate Active Listening:

Eliminate Distractions Provide your undivided attention by turning away from screens, muting notifications, and minimizing external distractions during conversations.

Use Reflective Listening: Paraphrase or summarize what you've heard to confirm your understanding and demonstrate that you've been paying attention.

Ask Open-ended Questions: Encourage further discussion and deeper insight by asking questions that require more than a yes/no answer.

Maintain Eye Contact: Eye contact conveys interest and helps you stay focused on the speaker.

Offer Feedback: Respond to what has been said with thoughtful comments or questions that show you're engaged and value the conversation.

Follow Up and Stay Connected

Following up and staying connected are pivotal steps in transforming fleeting encounters into enduring professional relationships. These steps ensure that the initial effort invested in networking cultivates a dynamic and supportive professional network.

A personalized follow-up message shortly after your initial meeting can make a lasting impression. Reference specific topics you discussed, express gratitude for the time spent, and perhaps suggest a future interaction if appropriate. This level of personalization shows that you were genuinely engaged in the conversation and value the connection, setting the stage for a relationship that extends beyond mere professional courtesy.

While email is a standard tool for follow-up, don't hesitate to use other platforms where appropriate. Social media, professional networking sites like LinkedIn, or even a handwritten note can add a personal touch to your message. The key is to choose the medium that best suits the nature of your relationship and the preferences of the person you're connecting with.

Ensure that your communications offer value to the recipient. This could be in the form of sharing an article relevant to a topic you discussed, providing a solution to a problem they mentioned, or introducing them to a contact who could help with their projects or career goals. Offering value reinforces the benefit of the connection and demonstrates your commitment to the relationship.

Actively monitor the progress and achievements of your connections and take the time to congratulate them on their milestones, whether it's a promotion, a successful project, or a personal accomplishment. Acknowledging their successes not only strengthens your relationship but also fosters a positive, supportive network culture.

Regular engagement keeps the connection alive, but it's essential to strike a balance that respects the other person's time and boundaries. Occasional check-ins, commenting on their public posts, or sharing insights that are genuinely of interest can maintain the connection without overwhelming them. The goal is to be present in their professional lives in a way that is supportive, not intrusive.

Networking is a long-term investment, and over time, some connections may become dormant. Periodically revisiting these contacts can rekindle valuable relationships. A simple message recalling your last interaction or noting a new common interest can reignite a conversation and potentially open doors to new opportunities or collaborations.

To effectively follow up and stay connected, consider scheduling regular reviews of your networking activities. This can involve going through your contacts to identify whom you haven't spoken to recently, who might benefit from an update you've come across, or who you could potentially introduce to each other. Such reviews help ensure no valuable connection falls through the cracks and your network remains vibrant and engaged.

Lastly, genuine relationships take time to develop. Approach each interaction with authenticity and patience, understanding that the fruits of networking may not be immediate but can yield significant benefits over time. Networking is as much about building a community as it is about advancing your career. By nurturing these connections with care and respect, you contribute to a professional ecosystem that is mutually supportive and enriching.

Practice and Reflect

Practicing and reflecting on your networking activities is a critical component of developing effective networking skills. Like any other skill, networking benefits immensely from deliberate practice and thoughtful reflection. This process not only enhances your ability to connect with others but also deepens your understanding of the dynamics of professional interactions.

Approach networking with the understanding that there's always room for growth and improvement. This mindset encourages you to see each interaction as a learning opportunity, regardless of its immediate outcome. By remaining open to learning, you position yourself to continuously enhance your networking skills and strategies.

Setting specific goals for your networking efforts can provide direction and a benchmark for measuring progress. These goals could range from expanding your network in a new industry, improving your small talk abilities, or becoming more effective at following up. Having clear objectives helps to focus your efforts and makes it easier to identify areas for improvement.

Networking can take many forms, from one-on-one meetings and group events to online interactions. Actively seek out a variety of networking situations to practice your skills. Each setting presents its own challenges and opportunities for learning. For example, engaging in online networking may hone your written communication skills, while attending live events can improve your ability to connect with strangers in a busy environment.

Feedback from peers or mentors can provide invaluable insights into your networking strengths and areas for improvement. Don't hesitate to ask for feedback from individuals you trust, especially if they've observed you in networking settings. They may offer perspectives on your approach that you hadn't considered, highlighting both your effective strategies and aspects you could refine.

After a networking interaction, take some time to reflect on how it went. Consider what went well and what could have been done differently. Did you achieve your objectives for the meeting? Were you able to establish a genuine connection? How effectively did you listen and respond? Reflecting on these questions can help you identify successful tactics and areas where you need more practice.

Mistakes are inevitable in any learning process, and networking is no exception. Instead of viewing missteps as failures, see them as valuable learning experiences. Analyse what went wrong and why, and consider how you can adjust your approach in the future to avoid similar pitfalls. This resilience in the face of setbacks is crucial for long-term improvement.

Based on your reflections and the feedback you receive, be willing to adjust your approach and experiment with new strategies. Networking styles are highly personal, and what works well for one person may not suit another. Experimenting with different techniques can help you discover what feels most natural and effective for you.

Finally, recognize and celebrate your progress, no matter how small. Networking can be challenging, especially for those who find social interactions daunting. Acknowledging your achievements, such as successfully initiating a conversation at a networking event or making a meaningful connection online, can provide motivation and reinforce the value of your efforts.

The 3 types of networking

Strategic Networking: Building Broader Connections for Organizational Growth

Leaders engage in strategic networking to extend their influence beyond their immediate professional circles. This form of networking is not just about personal career advancement; it's about forging connections that can benefit the organization as a whole. Strategic networking involves identifying and establishing relationships with key stakeholders, influencers, and decision-makers across different sectors or industries. The goal is to create a web of contacts that can offer insights, resources, and opportunities to support the organization's objectives and drive its mission forward.

The Industry Partnership Breakthrough Rahul, a partner in the consulting division of a Big4 firm, who attended an international finance conference. There, he strategically engaged with Elena, a C-suite executive from a global banking institution. Their conversation, intentionally steered by Rahul towards digital transformation in banking, unveiled shared interests and perspectives. This connection was no mere coincidence but a targeted effort by Rahul to find synergistic opportunities. Their discussion eventually led to a landmark partnership, where Rahul's firm provided the banking institution with cutting-edge consultancy on digital transformation, enhancing both entities' prestige and market position.

Anecdote 2: Influencing Policy through Thought Leadership Sarah, a senior consultant specializing in public sector projects, knew the importance of shaping policy to her consulting firm's advantage. She frequently organized roundtable discussions with policymakers, leveraging her firm's research to guide the conversations. Her strategic networking paid off when a policy advisory paper her team developed, influenced by these discussions, was adopted as a framework for regional economic development. This not only solidified her firm's reputation in public sector consultancy but also opened doors to new government contracts.

Leveraging LinkedIn for Thought Leadership Kevin, a director at a Big4 firm, mastered the art of using LinkedIn to amplify his and his firm's visibility in the industry. By curating insightful content, commenting on trends, and engaging with thought leaders' posts, Kevin positioned himself as a thought leader in regulatory compliance. His efforts culminated in a collaboration with a top regulatory technology company to develop a compliance solution, showcased in a series of highly attended webinars. This strategic move not only enhanced Kevin's stature but also brought his firm to the forefront of compliance consultancy.

Creating Academic Collaborations for Innovation Lina, who led a research team within a Big4 firm, saw the untapped potential in academic partnerships. She initiated collaborations with universities known for their cutting-edge research in artificial intelligence. By combining her team's industry knowledge with the academic world's innovative approaches, they co-developed AI solutions tailored to the needs of their clients. These partnerships not only accelerated the firm's R&D capabilities but also enriched the academic curriculum, showcasing a successful model of industry-academia collaboration in the consulting world.

Operational Networking

Operational networking focuses on building relationships that help leaders manage their internal responsibilities more effectively. This includes connecting with peers, subordinates, and superiors within the organization to streamline operations, facilitate problem-solving, and ensure the smooth execution of tasks. Operational networking is essential for gathering critical information, garnering support for initiatives, and fostering a collaborative work environment. By leveraging these internal connections, leaders can enhance organizational efficiency, navigate workplace dynamics, and lead more effectively.

Facilitating Seamless Integration of a New Service Line When Jasmine, a partner at a Big4 firm, was charged with integrating a new cybersecurity consulting service into the firm's existing offerings, she knew coordination across multiple departments was key. By leveraging her operational network, Jasmine organized a series of strategy sessions with leaders from IT, legal, marketing, and client service teams. These sessions ensured that every department was aligned with the integration process, identifying potential roadblocks and collaboratively developing solutions. Jasmine's proactive use of her internal network not only streamlined the service line integration but also fostered a stronger sense of unity and shared purpose across the firm.

Navigating Client Delivery Challenges through Internal Expertise Alex, a senior consultant facing a complex challenge with a high-profile client's project, realized the solution lay within the firm's vast pool of expertise. Utilizing his operational network, he quickly identified and collaborated with a colleague who had successfully managed a similar situation. This internal consultation allowed Alex to apply a proven strategy to his client's project, ensuring timely and effective resolution. His ability to tap into the firm's collective knowledge through operational networking underscored the power of internal collaboration in enhancing client service.

Gaining Buy-in for Organizational Transformation Lena, tasked with leading a digital transformation initiative within her consulting firm, understood the importance of internal buy-in for the project's success. Through her operational network, she engaged key stakeholders across the firm, from junior consultants to senior partners, in a series of interactive workshops. These discussions not only helped address concerns and suggestions but also turned potential sceptics into advocates for the transformation. Lena's strategic engagement of her operational network ensured widespread support, smoothing the path for the initiative's successful implementation.

Cross-functional Teams Driving Innovation Daniel, a director in a Big4 firm, saw the potential for innovation through cross-functional collaboration. He formed a task force combining talents from the strategy, technology, and human resources departments, all sourced through his operational networking efforts. This diverse team was charged with developing innovative approaches to talent management and client engagement. The collaborative effort led to the introduction of groundbreaking AI-driven tools for talent development and client interaction, showcasing the value of leveraging a diverse operational network to drive innovation within the firm.

Personal Networking: Developing Personal Growth and Professional Skills

Personal networking is centred around an individual's career development and personal growth. This type of networking is crucial for acquiring new skills, gaining insights into industry trends, and exploring career opportunities. Through personal networking, leaders can find mentors, seek advice, and receive feedback that is vital for their professional advancement. It's about building a diverse network of contacts from whom they can learn and with whom they can share experiences. Personal networking not only contributes to a leader's professional development but also enriches their personal life by providing support, inspiration, and a sense of community.

Finding a Mentor in Mergers and Acquisitions Amanda, a junior consultant with a keen interest in mergers and acquisitions (M&A), realized the importance of having a mentor to navigate her career path effectively. At a Big4 firm networking event, she connected with a senior partner known for his expertise in M&A. Amanda reached out for advice, which blossomed into a mentoring relationship. Through regular meetings, she gained invaluable insights into the nuances of M&A deals, learned about key industry trends, and developed strategies for her career progression. This mentorship not only accelerated Amanda's professional development but also provided her with a trusted advisor for navigating career decisions.

Leveraging Peer Networks for Skill Development Raj, an audit manager at a Big4 firm, was interested in enhancing his understanding of digital audit tools to stay ahead in his field. Recognizing the limitations of formal training programs, Raj turned to his personal network, organizing a peer learning group with colleagues across different departments who were also interested in digital innovations in auditing. Together, they shared resources, organized workshops, and invited experts for talks, creating a vibrant community of practice. This initiative not only bolstered Raj's expertise in digital audit tools but also fostered a culture of continuous learning within his network.

Gaining Industry Insights through Cross-industry Connections Sophia, a strategy consultant, understood the importance of staying informed about broader industry trends and their implications for her clients. She made it a point to attend industry conferences outside her consulting specialty, connecting with professionals in tech, healthcare, and finance. These cross-industry connections enriched her perspective, allowing her to bring fresh insights into her consulting projects. For instance, through a connection made at a fintech conference, Sophia was able to apply innovative financial technologies to a traditional banking client, significantly enhancing the project's outcome.

Navigating Career Transitions with Support from Professional Networks When Alex, a seasoned tax consultant at a Big4 firm, contemplated a transition into environmental sustainability consulting, he tapped into his personal network for guidance. Through conversations with contacts in sustainability roles, Alex gained a realistic understanding of the new field, including the challenges and opportunities it presented. These insights, combined with encouragement and practical advice from his network, equipped Alex to make a successful career pivot, illustrating the vital role of personal networking in navigating significant career transitions.

Chapter 4 – Acing the Interview

Landing an interview with a Big4 firm is an accomplishment in itself, marking the first significant milestone in your journey to securing a coveted position within these prestigious organizations. However, the interview stage is where the real challenge begins, demanding preparation, strategy, and a deep understanding of what these firms are looking for in their ideal candidates. This chapter is designed to be your comprehensive guide to acing the interview, transforming this daunting hurdle into an opportunity to shine and make an unforgettable impression.

The interview process at Big4 firms is notoriously rigorous, designed to test not only your technical skills and knowledge but also your problem-solving abilities, adaptability, and fit within the firm's culture. It's a crucible intended to distil the essence of your professional potential and personal ethos. Here, we'll dissect the interview process, offering insights into the various stages you may encounter, from the initial phone screen to the final round with senior partners.

First, we delve into the preparatory steps necessary to enter your interviews with confidence. This includes understanding the firm's core values and how they resonate with your personal and professional experiences. We'll guide you through crafting compelling stories that highlight your achievements, challenges overcome, and the lessons learned along the way. These narratives are the golden threads that will weave through your interview responses, making them memorable and impactful.

Next, we explore the specific types of questions you can expect, ranging from technical and competency-based inquiries to behavioural and case study questions. Each question type serves a distinct purpose, testing various facets of your candidacy. We provide strategies for tackling these questions, incorporating examples and frameworks to help you structure your responses effectively.

Furthermore, we recognize that the Big4 interview is not a one-way street. It's also an opportunity for you to assess the firm and determine if it's the right fit for your career aspirations. To this end, we offer advice on formulating insightful questions to ask your interviewers, demonstrating your depth of interest in the firm and the role you're applying for.

An essential aspect of acing the interview is mastering the non-verbal cues and communication skills that can significantly influence the interviewer's perception. From the firm handshake at the beginning to the poised demeanour throughout the interview, these subtle signals play a crucial role in conveying confidence and professionalism.

Finally, we address the post-interview phase, including best practices for follow-up communications that can keep you top of mind for the hiring managers. A thoughtful thank-you note or email can underscore your enthusiasm for the role and your attention to professional courtesies.

This chapter is more than just a guide; it's a roadmap to navigating the complex landscape of Big4 interviews with assurance and agility. By internalizing these insights and strategies, you'll be well-equipped to turn every question into an opportunity to showcase your strengths and every interaction into a step closer to your goal of joining a Big4 firm. Let's embark on this journey together, turning potential into performance, and aspirations into achievements.

Understanding the Firm's Core Values

The journey to securing a position within a Big4 firm is not solely about showcasing your technical skills or professional accolades; it's equally about demonstrating a deep alignment with the firm's core values. These prestigious firms are pillars of professionalism, integrity, and excellence, and they rigorously seek candidates who not only excel in their field but also embody the principles that define their corporate identity. Here's how you can delve into understanding and aligning with these core values to present yourself as the ideal candidate.

Researching the Firm's Mission and Values Start with a deep dive into the firm's foundational beliefs. Visit their official website, where these firms often articulate their mission statement, core values, and vision for the future. These values might range from commitment to excellence and integrity in client service to fostering an inclusive and supportive work environment. It's essential to grasp not just the wording but the essence of these values—how they inform the firm's decisions, strategies, and daily operations.

Analysing Recent Initiatives and Projects

Look beyond the mission statement to the firm's actions in the real world. This could involve significant projects, recent initiatives, community involvement, and how they address global challenges. For example, a firm might prioritize sustainability, launching initiatives to reduce its carbon footprint, or emphasize the importance of diversity and inclusion by supporting various community programs. These actions provide insight into what the firm values beyond its bottom line and how it enacts its principles in its business practices.

Embracing Sustainability Jordan, a prospective candidate, was deeply passionate about environmental sustainability. While researching a Big4 firm he wished to join, he discovered their commitment to becoming carbon neutral by 2030. The firm had invested in renewable energy projects and implemented policies to reduce its carbon footprint. Inspired by this, Jordan reflected on his own experience leading a sustainability initiative in his previous role, where he helped his company reduce energy consumption by implementing a new, eco-friendly technology stack. During his interview, he shared this story, drawing a parallel between his personal commitment to sustainability and the firm's ambitious environmental goals. This not only demonstrated his alignment with the firm's values but also showcased his proactive approach to making a positive impact.

Championing Diversity and Inclusion Samantha was impressed by a Big4 firm's initiative to support underrepresented communities in the tech industry. The firm had launched a mentorship program that paired its consultants with students from diverse backgrounds, aiming to bridge the gap in tech education. Samantha connected this with her volunteer experience as a mentor in a similar program, where she guided young women in STEM fields, providing career advice and support. During her networking sessions with the firm, she shared her experiences and the lessons learned about the importance of diversity and inclusion in creating innovative solutions. Her stories resonated with the firm's commitment, illustrating her genuine passion for fostering an inclusive environment.

Supporting Community Programs Alex discovered that the Big4 firm he aspired to join was actively involved in community support programs, particularly in response to the recent global health crisis. The firm had contributed significant resources to local healthcare systems and provided pro bono consulting to struggling small businesses. Alex had a similar experience when he initiated a community outreach program through his previous employer, offering free workshops and consultations to local entrepreneurs to help them digitalize their operations amid the pandemic. During his application process, Alex highlighted this initiative, emphasizing his belief in using his skills for the greater good and his alignment with the firm's community-focused values.

Reflecting on Value Alignment

With a clear understanding of the firm's values and actions, it's time to introspect and identify points of alignment with your own values and experiences. Perhaps you've led or participated in projects with a strong emphasis on sustainability, or maybe you've been active in initiatives that promote diversity and inclusion. Drawing parallels between your actions and the firm's values is crucial. This exercise isn't about forcing a fit; it's about highlighting genuine connections between your personal and professional ethos and the firm's core values.

Demonstrating Value Alignment in Your Application

Knowing the firm's values and recognizing your alignment with them is just the first step. The critical part is effectively communicating this alignment in your application, interviews, and interactions with the firm. Prepare to share specific anecdotes or examples from your career that demonstrate how you've lived these values in your professional journey. Whether it's a project where you went above and beyond to ensure client satisfaction or an initiative you led to improve team diversity, these stories can powerfully showcase your fit with the firm's culture.

Staying Authentic

While aligning with a firm's values is crucial, authenticity is key. Attempting to present yourself as a perfect fit by overstating your alignment can be counterproductive. Be honest about where your values strongly align with the firm's and where there might be differences. This honesty shows self-awareness and integrity, traits that are highly valued by Big4 firms.

Crafting Your Personal Narratives

Your resume lists your achievements, but it's the stories behind these bullet points that will capture the interviewer's attention. Think of challenges you've faced, milestones you've achieved, and lessons you've learned along the way. Structure these experiences into compelling narratives that demonstrate your resilience, adaptability, teamwork, leadership, and any other qualities that resonate with the firm's values. Use the STAR (Situation, Task, Action, Result) technique to give your stories structure, ensuring you convey a clear narrative arc that highlights your role and the impact of your actions.

Situation: Set the scene with enough context so the interviewer understands the background.

Task: Describe your responsibility in that situation.

Action: Elaborate on what you did, focusing on your individual contribution even if it was a team effort.

Result: Highlight the outcome of your actions, including what you learned from the experience.

The STARR technique is also useful when you encounter a particular type of interview question designed to probe into their professional history and behavioural patterns. These inquiries typically begin with prompts such as:

"Tell me about a time when..."

"Can you recall a situation in which..."

"Give me an example of a time when you..."

Known as behavioural interview questions, their purpose is to uncover insights into an applicant's previous work behaviours as predictors of their future performance. The STAR technique emerges as a vital strategy for navigating these questions, allowing for responses that are not only detailed and structured but also engaging for the interviewer.

Moreover, the utility of the STAR method extends beyond behavioural questions. It proves equally effective in articulating responses to a wide array of inquiries, whether discussing one's greatest achievements, challenges overcome, strengths demonstrated, or weaknesses acknowledged. The technique facilitates a storytelling approach that makes the candidate's examples more vivid and memorable.

Situational questions, which present hypothetical scenarios asking how a candidate might respond, also benefit from the integration of the STAR method. While these questions explore potential future actions rather than past experiences, incorporating the STAR structure can lend depth and credibility to responses. By briefly referencing a real-life example that mirrors the hypothetical situation, candidates can demonstrate how their past behaviours inform their decision-making processes.

Incorporating the STAR method into replies, especially when addressing hypothetical situations, enriches a candidate's answers with concrete evidence of their capabilities and problem-solving skills. It transforms abstract scenarios into opportunities to showcase real-world applications of their knowledge and experience.

Here are some examples that you can use:

Resilience in Crisis:

Situation: During a merger, our company faced integration challenges.

Task: As part of the HR team, my responsibility was to ensure a smooth transition for employees.

Action: I organized town hall meetings, addressed concerns, and provided emotional support.

Result: Morale improved, and employee retention increased. I learned resilience under pressure.

Adaptability in Change:

Situation: Our project scope expanded unexpectedly due to client demands.

Task: As a consultant, I needed to adapt quickly and reallocate resources.

Action: I restructured the project plan, communicated changes, and led the team through adjustments.

Result: We delivered ahead of schedule, exceeding client expectations. I learned agility.

Leadership in Crisis Management:

Situation: A major software glitch disrupted operations.

Task: As the tech lead, I had to resolve the issue swiftly.

Action: I coordinated a 24-hour debugging session, involving engineers from different time zones.

Result: We fixed the problem, minimizing downtime. I learned the value of decisive leadership.

Tailoring Stories to Different Themes

It's crucial to approach the interview process with a strategic mindset, particularly in the art of storytelling. The narratives you choose to share during your interview can significantly impact the impression you leave on your interviewers. Therefore, it's beneficial to meticulously prepare and tailor your stories to align with the various themes or competencies these firms typically seek in their candidates. Common areas of interest include leadership, problem-solving, ethical judgment, and client service, among others.

To effectively showcase your suitability for the role, it's advisable to curate a diverse collection of stories from your professional and personal experiences. This collection should vividly illustrate your abilities and achievements across the aforementioned competencies. By having a wide range of narratives at your disposal, you ensure that you can confidently respond to a variety of questions, demonstrating your versatility and depth as a candidate.

The process of tailoring your stories goes beyond mere preparation; it involves a deep reflection on your experiences, enabling you to identify and articulate the most relevant and impactful insights. This reflective practice not only enhances the quality of your responses but also signals to your interviewers your capacity for self-assessment and growth.

Moreover, adapting your stories to specifically address the question or theme presented by the interviewer demonstrates a high level of engagement and attentiveness. It shows that you're not just recounting rehearsed anecdotes but are actively applying your experiences in a way that is meaningful and relevant to the discussion at hand.

Leadership

Question or Theme Can you describe a situation where you had to lead a team through a challenging period?

Adapted Story Instead of giving a generic response about leadership qualities, you recount a specific project where you led your team through a tight deadline after a key member unexpectedly left. You detail how you redistributed tasks, motivated the team by setting clear goals, and increased communication to ensure everyone was aligned. This story demonstrates your leadership skills, your ability to navigate challenges, and how you keep your team focused under pressure.

Problem-Solving

Question or Theme Tell us about a time when you solved a complex problem.

Adapted Story Rather than providing a broad overview of your problem-solving skills, you share a specific instance where you identified a recurring issue in the company's supply chain that was causing delays. You explain how you analysed the supply chain process, identified the bottleneck, proposed a solution to automate part of the process, and worked with the team to implement it, ultimately saving time and reducing costs. This response showcases your analytical thinking, initiative, and impact on efficiency.

Ethical Judgment

Question or Theme Have you ever faced an ethical dilemma at work? How did you handle it?

Adapted Story You recount a situation where you discovered a discrepancy in financial reporting that, if ignored, would benefit the company in the short term but could lead to significant issues later. You describe your decision to bring this to the attention of your manager, your role in the investigation that followed, and how you advocated for transparency. This narrative highlights your integrity, ethical judgment, and commitment to doing what's right, even in the face of potential pushback.

Client Service

Question or Theme Describe a time you went above and beyond for a client.

Adapted Story Instead of vaguely talking about your dedication to clients, you detail a particular instance where you noticed a client was struggling to use your product effectively, risking their satisfaction and potential renewal. You illustrate how you proactively reached out, provided additional training, and even spearheaded a minor feature update to address their specific needs, leading to a renewal and an upsell. This story demonstrates your proactive approach, attention to client needs, and the ability to drive results through exceptional service.

Practicing Your Delivery

Mastering the delivery of your carefully crafted narratives is just as important as the stories themselves. After all, the impact of a story is significantly influenced by how it's told. To ensure your stories resonate with your interviewers and leave a lasting impression, it's crucial to practice delivering them aloud. This isn't about memorizing each word but rather becoming familiar enough with your stories that you can recount them naturally and compellingly.

Start by practicing in a comfortable environment, perhaps in front of a mirror or while recording yourself. This initial step allows you to become more conscious of your pacing, tone, and body language—key elements that can enhance your storytelling. Pay attention to your facial expressions, eye contact (even if it's just with your reflection), and gestures. These non-verbal cues can add depth to your narratives, making them more engaging and memorable.

However, practicing alone is just the beginning. The real magic happens when you bring a friend, mentor, or coach into your rehearsal process. Choose someone you trust and who can offer honest, constructive feedback. As you practice your stories with them, they can observe and comment on aspects you might overlook, such as the clarity of your message, the natural flow of your delivery, and how well you're using non-verbal communication to your advantage. They can also simulate the interview setting, asking you questions and providing prompts, which can help you adapt your stories to different themes or questions on the spot.

This collaborative practice serves multiple purposes. It not only helps you refine your delivery but also boosts your confidence. Receiving feedback and making adjustments based on it ensures that your stories are not just heard but felt by the listener. Your practice partner can also challenge you by interrupting or asking follow-up questions, preparing you for the dynamic nature of real interview.

Furthermore, this practice makes you more comfortable with the material, ensuring that during the actual interview, your stories don't sound rehearsed or robotic. Instead, they'll flow smoothly, reflecting your genuine experiences and personality. The goal is to reach a point where you can share your narratives with enthusiasm, authenticity, and a personal touch that captures the essence of who you are and what you bring to the table.

The initial interviews

with Big 4 firms (Deloitte, PwC, EY, and KPMG) often focuses on understanding the candidate's background, skills, and motivation. This stage is crucial for making a strong first impression and setting the tone for subsequent rounds. Here are typical questions you might encounter in a Stage 1 interview with a Big 4 firm, along with a brief explanation of what the interviewer might be looking for in your response:

Tell me about yourself.

"Tell me about yourself" is perhaps one of the most common yet crucial questions posed during interviews at the Big Four accounting firms—Deloitte, PwC, EY, and KPMG. This open-ended prompt provides a golden opportunity to frame your narrative, emphasizing how your experiences and achievements align with the values and needs of the firm.

The question serves multiple purposes: it allows interviewers to start the conversation, provides insight into your self-perception and priorities, and assesses your communication skills. Effective answers will succinctly connect your background to the specific requirements and culture of the firm.

A good structure to follow is the present-past-future formula:

Present: Start with where you are now in your career.

Past: Briefly touch on past experiences and proven achievements relevant to the position.

Future: Conclude with why you're excited about this opportunity.

Examples of Effective Responses

Example 1: Audit Associate Applicant

Present: "I am currently a junior auditor with two years of experience at a mid-sized firm where I handle a portfolio of clients in the retail and manufacturing sectors."

Past: "During my tenure, I've implemented a new analytical approach that improved our audit efficiency by 15% and reduced errors by 25%. This experience ignited my passion for leveraging technology to enhance accuracy and efficiency in auditing."

Future: "I'm eager to bring this passion and my hands-on experience to Deloitte, known for its innovative auditing services and commitment to professional development."

Example 2: Tax Consultant Applicant

Present: "I'm a tax consultant specializing in U.S. corporate tax law, currently working with a diverse range of multinational corporations."

Past: "Over the past three years, I've helped companies navigate complex tax reforms and saved them over $3 million in potential tax liabilities through strategic planning. My article on tax strategy for international mergers was published in 'The Tax Advisor' last year, which was a significant personal achievement."

Future: "I am looking to advance my career in a dynamic environment, where I can contribute to and learn from the best in the field, especially with your firm's strong focus on global tax challenges."

Tips for Personalizing Your Answer

Connect personally: Mention what personally drives you to work in this field or for the Big Four specifically. For instance, a deep-seated interest in corporate ethics, inspired by a university mentor or a specific course, can resonate well, especially for firms like these that value integrity.

Be concise and relevant: While it's tempting to share your entire career history, focus on what's most relevant to the position. Tailor your achievements to mirror the skills and experiences the firm values.

Practice your delivery: Your answer should be well-practiced but not memorized verbatim, ensuring it sounds natural and confident.

"Why do you want to work for us?"

The question "Why do you want to work for us?" is almost inevitable. This question tests your knowledge of the firm, your professional alignment with its values and goals, and your long-term career aspirations. Crafting a thoughtful and personalized answer can significantly impact the interviewer's perception of your fit for the firm.

This question helps interviewers gauge:

Your familiarity with the firm Understanding its services, culture, and industry standing.

Your professional alignment How the firm's goals and values resonate with your own career objectives.

Your commitment Demonstrating genuine interest in being part of the firm long-term.

Your response should reflect thorough research about the firm and link your skills and aspirations to what the firm offers. Here's a helpful structure:

Knowledge of the firm Highlight specific facts about the firm that appeal to you (innovations, culture, leadership, etc.).

Professional alignment Discuss how these aspects align with your career goals.

Personal connection and enthusiasm Conclude by expressing your eagerness to contribute to and grow with the firm.

Examples of Effective Responses

Example for Deloitte

Knowledge "Deloitte's commitment to leading in sustainability and climate change initiatives stands out in the industry. Your recent launch of the World Climate strategy is particularly inspiring."

Alignment "I have spent the past three years developing a sustainability audit framework that aligns closely with Deloitte's objectives in this area. My approach has helped several businesses implement more sustainable practices effectively."

Connection "I am eager to bring this experience to Deloitte, where I believe I can contribute to and expand on these pioneering initiatives."

Example for PwC

Knowledge "PwC's focus on digital transformation, especially your investments in artificial intelligence and blockchain, aligns with the future of financial services."

Alignment "My recent project involved creating an AI-driven tool that enhanced financial forecasting for clients by 30%. I am passionate about leveraging technology to solve complex business challenges."

Connection "Working at PwC would not only allow me to apply my skills on a larger scale but also keep me at the forefront of technological advancements in auditing and consulting."

Tips for Personalizing Your Answer

Do your homework Research recent news about the firm, read their annual report, and understand their strategic goals.

Be specific Mention specific programs, initiatives, or leaders that inspire you; avoid vague or generic statements.

Relate to your journey Connect your personal career path or key achievements directly to the firm's work or values.

What do you know about our services and clients?

This question assesses your understanding of the firm's offerings and its market. Highlight your knowledge of the firm's services, any notable clients (without violating confidentiality if you're aware of them through your network), and recent news or projects that caught your attention.

Can you describe a challenging situation you faced and how you dealt with it?

A classic behavioural question aimed at assessing your problem-solving and resilience. Use the STAR method (Situation, Task, Action, Result) to structure your answer, emphasizing the actions you took and the outcome.

How do you work in a team? Can you give an example of a successful team project?

Big 4 firms highly value teamwork and collaboration. Share an experience that showcases your ability to work effectively with others, your role in the team, and the success achieved collectively.

What are your strengths and weaknesses?

Be honest but strategic; choose strengths that are relevant to the job and discuss weaknesses that you're actively working to improve. Illustrate with examples where possible.

Where do you see yourself in five years?

This question gauges your ambition, career planning, and whether your long-term goals align with the company's growth opportunities. Be realistic but show enthusiasm for progressing within the firm.

How do you manage deadlines and prioritize tasks?

Time management is crucial in the fast-paced environment of Big 4 firms. Describe your approach to prioritizing work and give examples of how you've managed competing deadlines in the past.

Describe a time when you had to handle feedback.

This question assesses your receptiveness to feedback and ability to adapt and grow. Share a specific instance when you received constructive feedback, how you responded, and the positive changes that resulted.

Why should we hire you?

Summarize your key qualifications, experiences, and traits that make you a great fit for the position. Highlight what sets you apart from other candidates and how you can contribute to the firm.

The technical interview

This interview is designed to assess your specific skill set and expertise relevant to the role you're applying for. This could range from accounting and audit practices to consulting methodologies, tax legislation, or IT knowledge, depending on the position. Unlike the initial interview, which focuses more on your general competencies and behavioural traits, the technical interview dives into your professional acumen. Here's how to prepare for it effectively:

Understand the Job Description

Review the Role Start by thoroughly reviewing the job description. Understand the technical skills and knowledge areas listed as requirements or preferences for the role.

Identify Key Topics Based on the job description, identify key topics and areas that are likely to be covered in the technical interview.

Brush Up on Fundamental Concepts

Refresh Your Knowledge Revisit fundamental concepts, standards, and methodologies relevant to your field. For an accounting position, this might include GAAP or IFRS principles; for IT roles, programming languages or cybersecurity principles.

Stay Updated Make sure you're up to date with the latest trends, technologies, regulations, and best practices in your industry.

IN MY TECHNICAL INTERVIEWS, I VEERED AWAY FROM PURELY TECHNICAL QUESTIONS, AS IT'S TOO EASY TO CATCH A CANDIDATE OFF GUARD WITH OBSCURE QUERIES. INSTEAD, I OPTED FOR MORE OPEN-ENDED QUESTIONS. FOR INSTANCE, I MIGHT ASK HOW A CANDIDATE WOULD

HANDLE A SCENARIO WHERE, LATE ONE EVENING, WHILE WORKING TOWARDS A TIGHT DEADLINE FOR A CHALLENGING CUSTOMER, THEY ENCOUNTER A SOFTWARE DEFECT. THIS ALLOWED ME TO GAUGE THEIR UNDERSTANDING OF PROJECT GOVERNANCE, COLLABORATION, AND EFFECTIVE COMMUNICATION.

ANOTHER FAVORED APPROACH OF MINE WAS ROLE-PLAYING A SITUATION WHERE I ACTED AS THE CUSTOMER INSISTING ON SOMETHING THAT WASN'T BEST PRACTICE. HERE, I ASSESSED THE CANDIDATE'S ABILITY TO GRASP THE REAL REQUIREMENTS, TACTFULLY SUGGEST ALTERNATIVES, AND ARTICULATE WHY THESE ALTERNATIVES WERE SUPERIOR TO WHAT THE CUSTOMER WANTED.

I PROBED BOTH AREAS OF STRENGTH AND WEAKNESS. I DIDN'T PENALIZE A CANDIDATE FOR NOT KNOWING A VERY SPECIFIC PIECE OF FUNCTIONALITY THAT COULD EASILY BE GOOGLED, AS LONG AS THEY HAD A SOLID GRASP OF CORE FUNCTIONS. EXPLORING AREAS OF WEAKNESS IN KNOWLEDGE PROVIDED INSIGHTS INTO HOW THE CANDIDATE WOULD HANDLE SIMILAR SITUATIONS WITH A CUSTOMER—IT WAS MORE ABOUT THEIR ABILITY TO DEMONSTRATE RESOURCEFULNESS.

HERE'S A SAMPLE QUESTION (SAP-RELATED, AS THAT WAS MY DOMAIN):

"YOU'RE IN A WORKSHOP, AND TWO CUSTOMER IT RESOURCES ARE ARGUING ABOUT THE TECHNICAL ARCHITECTURE. ONE WANTS TO USE SAP ANALYTICS CLOUD DIRECTLY CONNECTED TO AZURE, WHILE THE OTHER INSISTS ON SAP BW/4HANA. YOU'RE TASKED WITH WRITING THE ANALYTICS STRATEGY DOCUMENT. WHAT WOULD YOU ADVISE THE CUSTOMER?"

Practical Experience

Draw from Real-World Scenarios Be prepared to discuss how you've applied technical knowledge in practical situations. Think of specific projects or tasks where you've demonstrated your technical skills.

Problem-Solving Examples Have examples ready that showcase your problem-solving abilities, where you applied technical knowledge to overcome challenges.

Practice and Research

Mock Interviews Conduct mock interviews focusing on technical questions with a peer or mentor. This can help simulate the pressure of the real interview.

Research the Firm Understand how the firm utilizes technology and technical skills in its services. This insight can help you tailor your responses to fit the firm's context and needs.

Prepare to Explain Complex Information

Simplify Complex Concepts Practice explaining complex technical concepts in a clear, concise manner. You may need to convey technical information to interviewers who might not share your expertise.

Stay Structured

Use Frameworks For case studies or complex problem-solving questions, employ structured frameworks to organize your thoughts and communicate your approach clearly.

Prepare Questions

Inquire About Applications Prepare to ask questions about how the firm applies certain technologies or methodologies in its projects. This shows your interest and eagerness to learn.

Mindset and Attitude

Adaptability Show that you're adaptable and eager to learn. Firms are looking for candidates who can grow and evolve with industry changes.

Confidence and Humility: Approach your technical interview with confidence in your skills and experience, but be open to acknowledging areas where you have room to grow.

The final interview at a Big 4 firm is a critical juncture in the recruitment process, where the firm assesses if you're the right fit for their team and culture. This stage often involves meeting with senior members of the firm, such as partners or directors, and can cover a wide range of topics from your personal and professional qualifications to how well you align with the firm's values and future direction. Here are some strategic hints on how to prepare for this pivotal moment:

Deep Dive into the Firm's Culture and Values

Research Thoroughly Understand the core values, mission, and culture of the firm. Look into their latest projects, achievements, and any CSR initiatives they're involved in. Demonstrating knowledge about the firm's ethos and how you align with it can significantly impact the interview's outcome.

Reflect on Your Journey and Aspirations

Personal and Professional Alignment Be prepared to discuss how your career goals align with the opportunities the firm offers. Reflect on your journey, highlighting experiences that showcase your growth, resilience, and readiness for the challenges this role might present.

Prepare for a Conversation Beyond the Resume

Broad Scope of Topics While technical skills are crucial, the final interview often delves into areas beyond the specifics of your professional expertise. Be ready to engage in discussions about industry trends, your perspectives on future challenges, and how you envision contributing to the firm's success.

Understand the Big Picture

Strategic Fit Think about what you bring to the table not just in terms of job performance but also how you would fit into the team and contribute to the firm's long-term goals. Be prepared to articulate your vision of how you can impact the firm beyond the immediate role.

Practice Your Storytelling

Engaging Narratives Have a set of compelling stories from your experience that illustrate your skills, values, and character. Use the STAR method (Situation, Task, Action, Result) to structure your stories in a way that is engaging and highlights your contributions and outcomes.

Prepare Thoughtful Questions

Show Your Engagement The final interview is also your opportunity to ask questions. Prepare thoughtful questions that demonstrate your interest in the firm and the role. Inquire about challenges, team dynamics, or the firm's vision for the future.

Exhibit Soft Skills

Communication and Emotional Intelligence Pay attention to your non-verbal cues and actively listen during the conversation. Demonstrating emotional intelligence and the ability to communicate effectively is key, especially for roles that involve client interaction or team leadership.

Final Preparations

Logistics and Mindset Ensure you know the interview's format, whether virtual or in-person, and plan accordingly. Approach the interview with a confident, positive mindset, ready to showcase why you are the ideal candidate for the firm.

Aligning Personal Goals with Firm's Objectives

Aligning your personal career goals with the objectives of the firm you're aiming to join is a crucial step in preparing for your Big 4 interviews. This alignment demonstrates to your interviewers that you've thought deeply about how this role and company fit into your larger professional trajectory. It's about showing that your ambitions dovetail with the direction the firm is headed, indicating a mutual benefit to your employment there. Let's explore how to effectively communicate this alignment and why it matters.

Understand the Firm's Objectives Begin by conducting thorough research on the firm's current projects, its strategic direction, and core values. For instance, if you're applying to a firm known for its innovation in sustainability within financial services, and you have a passion for environmental causes and a background in finance, this is a perfect alignment to highlight.

Articulate Your Career Aspirations Reflect on your long-term career goals and how the role you're applying for serves as a stepping stone towards those goals. For example, if your aspiration is to become an expert in tax advisory for multinational corporations and the firm is a leader in this area, explain how this role is aligned with your professional growth plan.

Provide Specific Examples When discussing your ambitions, be specific. Say something like, "My goal is to lead a team that drives technological innovations in audit processes. I've been following your firm's advancements in audit technology closely and am excited about the opportunity to contribute to these initiatives." This shows not only alignment but also initiative and engagement with the firm's work.

Discuss Growth Opportunities Talk about how the firm's culture of continuous learning and professional development can help you achieve your goals. For instance, mention your interest in taking advantage of their renowned training programs or your excitement about the potential to work on cross-functional teams that the firm encourages.

Show Commitment Express your commitment to not just joining the firm but growing with it. Highlight your desire to contribute to the firm's long-term success while also achieving your personal professional objectives. For example, you might say, "I am particularly drawn to your firm's approach to fostering long-term client relationships, and I see a great opportunity here to develop my skills in client management and strategic consulting, areas I am keen to excel in."

By connecting your personal professional aspirations with the firm's objectives, you make a compelling case for your candidacy. This alignment shows interviewers that you're not only a fit for the role based on your skills and experiences but also based on your vision for your future and the future of the firm. It illustrates foresight, a deep understanding of the firm's values and direction, and a commitment to contributing meaningfully to its growth. Entering your Big 4 interviews with this level of preparation and perspective not only sets you apart as a candidate but also ensures that you are making an informed and strategic decision about your career path.

Chapter 5: Cultural Adaptation

Landing a dream job at a Big 4 firm in the heart of London is an exciting prospect. However, it's not just your impressive technical abilities and stellar professional track record that will pave the way to success. Adapting to the cultural landscape of these esteemed firms, especially in a city as diverse as London, plays an equally crucial role. This chapter is your guide to seamlessly blending into the Big 4's vibrant and varied environment, ensuring you're not just a part of the team but a valued member who contributes to its rich cultural tapestry.

London's work culture, especially within the Big 4, is a melting pot of traditions, practices, and interactions. Understanding and navigating these nuances can make all the difference. We're here to walk you through what it takes to overcome any cultural barriers you might face, ensuring your transition is as smooth as possible.

Traditionally, the Big Four firms have placed a significant emphasis on conformity, the capacity to assimilate seamlessly into the firm's culture, and the readiness to dedicate long hours to work, all while upholding a robust ethic of client service. This set of characteristics has historically been seen as crucial to achieving career success within these organizations. Furthermore, the professional standards and practices within these firms have often been critiqued for reflecting a predominantly white, masculine, and patriarchal bias.

However, a notable shift is underway within the Big Four, signalling a profound transformation in the professional identity espoused by these firms. Particularly visible across various social media platforms, this shift marks a deliberate move away from the past's homogeneity towards a future where diversity and inclusiveness are not just welcomed but actively embraced. This evolution in perspective is not merely a surface-level change but indicates a deeper commitment to redefining what success looks like within these firms, making room for a broader range of voices, backgrounds, and experiences. This change reflects an understanding that embracing a rich tapestry of perspectives is crucial to fostering innovation, enhancing client service, and creating a more equitable and inclusive workplace.

First up, we'll dive into the heart of British workplace norms. If you're new to the UK or looking to refine your cultural intuition, this section is tailor-made for you. We'll explore everything from the art of mastering understated communication to the social intricacies that come with a tea break. It's about getting comfortable with the subtleties that define the professional landscape here.

Communication and teamwork take on a new dimension in a diverse setting like London's Big 4 firms. Being able to express your ideas with clarity, while respecting and understanding the perspectives of colleagues from around the globe, is key. This part of the chapter offers practical tips on boosting your communication skills and working collaboratively within multicultural teams. It's all about fostering an environment where everyone feels heard, respected, and valued.

Mastering British Workplace Norms

Welcome to the fascinating world of British workplace norms, a blend of tradition, formality, and understated communication that forms the backbone of professional life in the UK. Whether you're taking your first steps into the British corporate scene or simply keen to polish your understanding of its nuances, this section is designed to guide you through the unique aspects of working in the UK. Let's unravel the tapestry of customs and practices that could help you navigate your professional journey with confidence and ease.

The Art of Understated Communication

British communication is renowned for its subtlety and indirectness, where what is left unsaid can often be as important as the words spoken. Learning to navigate this can be key to effective workplace interactions. Phrases like "That's an interesting point" or "I'll bear it in mind" are polite ways of expressing scepticism or disagreement without direct confrontation. This nuanced communication style values the ability to read between the lines, understanding that feedback or suggestions are often delivered in a gentle, understated manner. Mastering this art can help you communicate more effectively with your colleagues and navigate workplace discussions with finesse.

The Social Intricacies of Tea Breaks

The humble tea break is a staple of British office life, serving not just as a brief respite in the day but as a pivotal social ritual. These moments offer a chance to bond with colleagues, discuss ideas informally, or simply catch up on office news. Participating in tea breaks can be a valuable way to integrate into the team and understand the office dynamics better. Remember, it's about more than just tea; it's an opportunity to connect on a personal level with those you work with daily.

Navigating Formality and Politeness

Despite the trend towards more casual business environments globally, the UK workplace maintains a certain level of formality. This is evident in the use of titles and surnames until invited to use first names, and in the structured approach to meetings and correspondence. Politeness is paramount, with "please," "thank you," and "sorry" being key components of workplace etiquette. Understanding and adopting this formal politeness can help in making positive impressions and building professional relationships.

The Importance of Punctuality

Punctuality is highly valued in the British workplace, often seen as a sign of respect and reliability. Being on time for meetings, appointments, and even casual work gatherings is important. It communicates your commitment and respect for others' time. If you're running late, notifying the relevant people as soon as possible is considered good etiquette.

Embracing the Pub Culture

The British pub culture extends into the professional world, with pubs often being the go-to venues for team celebrations, farewells, or Friday night drinks. These gatherings are an integral part of workplace social life, offering a relaxed environment to strengthen bonds with colleagues. Participation, while not mandatory, can be a great way to show team spirit and engage with your peers outside the office setting.

Effective communication and teamwork in a diverse environment

Landing a job at one of the Big Four accounting firms—Deloitte, PwC, EY, or KPMG—requires more than just technical expertise and a stellar resume; it demands exceptional interpersonal skills. In this chapter, we will explore the nuances of effective communication and teamwork in a diverse environment, a critical aspect of working at these global powerhouses. The Big Four firms are not just diverse in terms of the industries they serve but also in the cultural, educational, and professional backgrounds of their employees. Thriving in such an environment requires an understanding of diversity and the ability to communicate and collaborate effectively across various dimensions.

Understanding Diversity in the Big Four

Diversity in the Big Four extends beyond race and gender to encompass different thinking styles, cultural backgrounds, educational paths, and life experiences. Each employee brings a unique perspective that can contribute to innovative solutions and improved client service. Recognizing and valuing these differences is the first step toward effective teamwork.

Cultural Competence

Cultural competence is an essential skill for employees at the Big Four accounting firms. These global organizations operate across different countries and cultures, making it imperative for their employees to navigate and respect diverse cultural landscapes. Cultural competence not only promotes inclusivity but also enhances team collaboration and client relationships.

What is Cultural Competence?

Cultural competence involves understanding, respecting, and appropriately responding to the cultural differences that influence the behaviours of colleagues and clients. It includes knowledge of cultural customs, communication styles, and business practices that are distinct to different regions or ethnic groups. Developing cultural competence enables professionals to work more effectively in diverse teams and serve clients from various backgrounds. Here are some practical examples of Cultural Competence that I have come across during my time at a Big4:

Global Virtual Teams

Scenario: A team is working on a multinational project involving members from the United States, India, Japan, and Brazil. The project manager, based in the U.S., schedules weekly meetings without considering the local holidays of other countries, leading to frustrations and missed meetings.

Cultural Competence Application: Recognizing this oversight, the project manager consults an intercultural calendar and sets future meetings at times accommodating all team members' national holidays and working hours. This action demonstrates respect for each member's cultural context and improves participation and morale.

Client Presentations

Scenario: A team is preparing a business proposal for a potential client in the Middle East. The team plans to send a mixed-gender group to present the proposal.

Cultural Competence Application: Prior to the visit, the team participates in a workshop on Middle Eastern business etiquette. They learn about gender interaction norms in professional settings within the region. As a result, they adjust their presentation team and approach to align with the client's cultural expectations, which significantly enhances the client's comfort level and receptivity to the proposal.

Demonstrating Cultural Competence

Case Study 1: Cross-Cultural Mentoring Program

Background: EY implemented a cross-cultural mentoring program where senior leaders mentor employees from different cultural backgrounds. This initiative aims to foster understanding and build a supportive workplace environment.

Outcome: The program led to increased retention rates among minority groups and improved team collaboration. Mentors reported a deeper understanding of cultural challenges faced by their mentees, enabling them to advocate more effectively for inclusive policies and practices.

Case Study 2: PwC's Cultural Awareness Training

Background: PwC developed a series of cultural awareness training sessions designed to equip its workforce with the skills needed to navigate diverse cultural landscapes effectively. These sessions included case studies, role-playing exercises, and guest speakers from various cultural backgrounds.

Outcome: Employees who participated in the training showed greater sensitivity in their communications and were more adept at managing multicultural teams. The training also helped PwC enhance its client service in diverse markets, leading to an increase in client satisfaction scores.

Cognitive Diversity

Cognitive diversity refers to the inclusion of people who have different styles of problem-solving and can offer unique perspectives based on distinct ways of thinking. In the context of the Big Four accounting firms—Deloitte, PwC, EY, and KPMG—cognitive diversity is a crucial asset that enhances creative solutions and boosts overall team performance, especially when tackling complex, multifaceted business challenges.

Understanding Cognitive Diversity

Cognitive diversity can include differences in:

Problem-solving approaches: Some people prefer analytical methods, while others might choose more intuitive strategies.

Decision-making processes: Differences in risk assessment, priority setting, and the influence of past experiences.

Educational backgrounds: Varied academic disciplines can lead to different perspectives on the same issue.

Work experiences: Diverse professional experiences can influence how individuals approach tasks and solutions.

Embracing these varied perspectives can lead to more innovative solutions and is especially valuable in environments that require cross-functional collaboration. Here are some practical examples of cognitive diversity that I have come across:

Innovative Problem-Solving

Scenario: A team is tasked with developing a new risk management strategy for a client in the fintech sector. The team includes a statistician, a former banker, a cybersecurity expert, and a behavioural psychologist.

Cognitive Diversity Application: The statistician provides quantitative analysis, the banker offers insights into industry norms, the cybersecurity expert addresses potential security flaws, and the psychologist analyses how user behaviour might impact risk factors. The combined efforts lead to a comprehensive and robust risk management strategy that is innovative and well-rounded.

Product Development

Scenario: An innovation lab is working on an AI-based tool to improve audit processes. The team consists of AI researchers, audit specialists, software developers, and user experience designers.

Cognitive Diversity Application: The AI researchers propose cutting-edge algorithms, the audit specialists ensure the tool meets sector-specific needs, the software developers focus on integration and scalability, and the designers make sure the tool is user-friendly. The diverse expertise leads to the creation of a product that is technically advanced, practical, and easy to use.

Demonstrating Cognitive Diversity

Case Study 1: PwC's Think Tank Sessions

Background: PwC established a series of think tank sessions where employees from different departments come together to solve client problems. These sessions include people from tax, advisory, assurance, and legal services.

Outcome: These think tank sessions have led to several innovative solutions, such as a new tax optimization strategy that integrates legal and financial planning, benefiting clients with complex corporate structures. These solutions have been highly appreciated by clients for their creativity and effectiveness.

Case Study 2: EY's Digital Transformation Projects

Background: EY tackles digital transformation projects by assembling teams that include data scientists, management consultants, and sector-specific experts.

Outcome: For a healthcare client, this diverse team developed a digital health platform that not only leveraged data analytics for predictive care but also incorporated change management strategies to ensure adoption by healthcare providers. The project was notably successful, improving patient outcomes and operational efficiency.

Developing Effective Communication Skills

Effective communication is the backbone of successful teams, particularly in diverse settings where misunderstandings can arise easily. Here are strategies to enhance your communication skills in a Big Four context:

Active Listening

Listen to understand, not to respond. This involves paying attention to the speaker, asking clarifying questions, and reflecting back what you have heard to ensure understanding.

Clarity and Conciseness

Be clear and concise in your communications. Avoid jargon and be mindful of cultural nuances that might affect how your message is received.

Openness and Respect

Foster an environment where team members feel safe to express their ideas and opinions. This encourages dialogue and helps uncover hidden insights.

Feedback

Provide constructive feedback in a respectful manner. Likewise, be open to receiving feedback as a way to grow and improve.

Mastering Teamwork Dynamics

In the Big Four, you'll often work on teams that form and disband as projects start and finish. Being able to quickly adapt and function effectively within various teams is a valuable skill.

Building Trust and Inclusion

Trust Build trust by demonstrating reliability, integrity, and respect for your colleagues' expertise.

Inclusion Actively involve all team members in discussions and decision-making processes. Ensure that everyone feels valued and heard.

Leveraging Team Strengths

Identify and utilize the strengths of each team member. This not only boosts team efficiency but also helps individuals feel recognized and appreciated.

Managing Conflicts

Learn to manage and resolve conflicts constructively. Address issues directly and privately, seek to understand all perspectives, and work toward a solution that all parties can agree on.

Practical Tips for Thriving in a Diverse Team at a Big Four Firm

Understanding and respecting the cultural backgrounds of colleagues can significantly enhance teamwork, communication, and overall workplace harmony. Here are some practical tips and examples that illustrate the importance of cultural awareness in these settings.

Learn to Pronounce Names Correctly

Taking the time to learn and correctly pronounce the names of your colleagues is a fundamental sign of respect. It shows attentiveness and appreciation for the individual's identity, which can strengthen professional relationships. At PwC, a new manager made an effort to learn the correct pronunciation of all team members' names, particularly those that were non-Western. He used phonetic spellings in his contacts list to help remember the correct pronunciations. This effort did not go unnoticed and led to increased trust and openness within his team. The manager reported that such attention to detail helped in creating a more inclusive and respectful team environment.

Understand Basic Cultural Do's and Don'ts

Each culture has its unique set of norms and etiquettes. Being aware of these can prevent potential misunderstandings and offenses, which is crucial in maintaining a positive and productive work environment. A team from Deloitte was working on a merger project involving a company in Japan. One of the American team members learned that exchanging business cards is a ritual of significant importance in Japanese culture. Prior to their first meeting, he practiced the proper way to give and receive cards with both hands and a slight bow. This small act of cultural respect improved the rapport with their Japanese counterparts, facilitating smoother negotiations.

Celebrate Cultural Events

Acknowledging and celebrating the cultural events of different team members can enhance inclusivity and show that the organization values diversity. EY hosts an annual "Global Diversity Month" where they celebrate diverse cultural holidays and traditions from around the world. Each office organizes events and activities that highlight these traditions, such as food fairs, cultural performances, and presentations. These events not only educate employees about diverse cultures but also provide a platform for celebrating the diverse backgrounds of their workforce.

> DELOITTE IS KNOWN FOR HOSTING CULTURAL DIVERSITY EVENTS THROUGHOUT THE YEAR WITHIN ITS VARIOUS DIVISIONS. THESE EVENTS PROVIDE OPPORTUNITIES FOR COLLEAGUES FROM AROUND THE WORLD TO SHARE AND DISCUSS THEIR CULTURAL HERITAGE IN AN INFORMAL SETTING. I DISCOVERED THAT THESE EVENTS NOT ONLY HELPED ME UNDERSTAND MY COWORKERS' BACKGROUNDS AND FRAMES OF REFERENCE BETTER BUT ALSO FACILITATED CONNECTIONS AND NETWORKING. WE EMPHASIZED HOLDING THESE MEETINGS IN PERSON ONLY, WITH A DINNER AFTERWARD TO ENCOURAGE FURTHER INFORMAL CONVERSATIONS.

Engage in Cultural Training

Formal training can provide employees with a deeper understanding of cultural differences and how these can impact business practices and team dynamics. KPMG offers a series of cultural competence workshops that cover topics such as cross-cultural communication, international business etiquette, and managing multicultural teams. These workshops are particularly helpful for employees who work with international clients or in global teams. For example, after attending a workshop on Middle Eastern business practices, a consultant used his new knowledge to adjust his approach in a project proposal for a Saudi client, aligning with local business norms and expectations, which significantly enhanced the client relationship.

Flexibility and Adaptability

In the dynamic and diverse environment of the Big Four accounting firm's flexibility and adaptability are essential qualities for success. These skills enable professionals to navigate various client demands, cultural differences, and rapidly changing market conditions effectively. Below, we explore practical examples and anecdotes that demonstrate the importance of these traits in real-world settings within these organizations.

Adjusting Communication Styles

Adapting communication styles to match the preferences and cultural backgrounds of team members or clients can significantly enhance understanding and cooperation.

At Deloitte, a senior consultant was leading a team with members from different parts of the world, including Europe, Asia, and North America. She noticed that her direct and concise American communication style was causing misunderstandings with her Asian colleagues, who were used to more indirect expressions and formalities. Recognizing this, she began to incorporate more context into her communications and allowed more time for questions and clarifications in meetings. This adjustment helped improve team dynamics and project outcomes. The team members expressed greater satisfaction with their interactions, leading to more collaborative and efficient project execution.

Adapting Work Methods

Different situations may require different approaches to work, whether it's shifting deadlines, changing project scopes, or varying client expectations.

A PwC team working on a tax advisory project for a multinational corporation faced a sudden change when the client acquired another company, significantly altering the project's scope. Instead of sticking to their original plan, the team leader proposed a flexible approach, restructuring the team to include new experts in international tax law and merger regulations. This adaptability not only met the client's new needs but also demonstrated PwC's capacity to handle complex, evolving situations, thereby strengthening the client relationship.

Embracing New Technologies

The Big Four firms are at the forefront of incorporating innovative technologies into their services. Being adaptable includes being open to learning and integrating modern technologies into one's workflow.

At EY, an audit team was introduced to a new AI-driven analytics platform designed to enhance audit efficiency and accuracy. Initially, some team members were hesitant to adopt this new technology, preferring traditional methods. However, after a series of training sessions and seeing the benefits of the new system in speeding up data analysis and reducing errors, the team fully embraced the technology. This not only improved their performance on the audit but also prepared them for future projects where such advanced tools would be essential.

Handling Unexpected Challenges

Projects rarely go exactly as planned, and unexpected challenges can arise. Being flexible and adaptable allows team members to handle these situations effectively without derailing the project.

During a KPMG advisory project, a team was faced with unexpected regulatory changes that impacted their client's industry just weeks before the project's deadline. The team leader convened an emergency meeting to brainstorm solutions, adapting their strategy to address the new regulations. They also extended work hours and re-prioritized their milestones to ensure they met the deadline. Their ability to quickly adapt under pressure not only saved the project but also demonstrated their commitment and resilience to the client.

In conclusion, landing a dream job at a Big 4 firm in London is an incredible achievement that marks the beginning of a challenging yet rewarding journey. Success in these prestigious firms demands not only exceptional technical skills and a robust professional background but also the ability to seamlessly integrate into their diverse and dynamic work culture. By understanding and embracing British workplace norms, mastering the art of subtle communication, and engaging in social rituals such as tea breaks and pub outings, you can navigate the cultural landscape with confidence and ease.

Moreover, effective communication and teamwork in a multicultural environment are essential. Developing cultural competence, recognizing and valuing cognitive diversity, and fostering inclusive and collaborative team dynamics are crucial for thriving in the Big 4 setting. Practical examples and case studies from within these firms highlight the importance of these skills in enhancing team performance and client satisfaction.

Flexibility and adaptability further underline the capacity to respond to changing circumstances, client demands, and technological advancements. Embracing these qualities ensures you remain resilient and effective in a fast-paced, evolving industry.

Ultimately, your journey at a Big 4 firm is about more than just fitting in; it's about contributing to and benefiting from a rich tapestry of diverse perspectives and practices. By embracing these principles, you not only advance your career but also help shape a more inclusive and innovative future within these esteemed organizations.

Chapter 6: Career Growth and Development

Long-term Career Paths within the Big 4

A career at a Big 4 firm—Deloitte, PwC, EY, or KPMG—offers a structured yet dynamic pathway for professional growth. Each firm provides a clear career progression framework, but the opportunities for advancement and diversification are vast. Here's an overview of typical career paths and potential long-term trajectories within these firms:

Entry-Level Positions

Internships and Graduate Programs Many professionals start their journey with internships or graduate programs. These positions offer valuable exposure to the firm's culture, processes, and clients, often leading to full-time employment.

An intern or graduate in a Big 4 firm typically experiences a steep learning curve. Their day often starts with a team meeting where they receive assignments ranging from data entry and research to assisting with financial statement preparations. Throughout the day, they might shadow senior colleagues, attend training sessions, and help compile reports for client meetings. It's not unusual for interns to work long hours during peak periods, sometimes extending beyond the standard 9-to-5, especially during audit season or project deadlines. Despite the demanding schedule, the exposure to real-world business problems and the mentorship received are invaluable for their career development.

Associate/Analyst As entry-level roles, associates and analysts support senior staff in various tasks, including audits, tax preparations, consulting projects, and client interactions. This stage focuses heavily on learning and skill development.

Associates and analysts typically juggle multiple tasks daily, from conducting fieldwork at client sites to preparing audit documentation or financial analyses. They collaborate closely with senior associates and managers, often working under tight deadlines to ensure project deliverables are met. A significant part of their day might be spent on detailed data analysis, client correspondence, and ensuring compliance with regulatory standards. Working hours can be extensive, particularly during audit peaks or major project milestones, reflecting the high-paced environment of the Big 4.

Mid-Level Positions

Senior Associate/Senior Analyst After gaining a few years of experience, professionals move into senior roles, taking on more complex assignments, leading smaller projects, and mentoring junior staff.

Senior associates and senior analysts have more responsibility and autonomy. They often lead smaller projects and oversee the work of junior staff, providing guidance and feedback. Their day might include client meetings to present findings, conducting in-depth reviews of audit files, and managing project timelines and budgets. Senior roles also involve mentoring and training junior staff, helping them navigate their tasks and develop their skills. While the hours can still be long, senior associates generally have more control over their schedules and tasks, balancing client demands with team management responsibilities.

Manager Managers oversee multiple projects and are responsible for client relationships, project management, and team supervision. This role requires a strong balance of technical expertise and leadership skills.

A manager's day is highly varied and demanding. They are often involved in high-level client interactions, project planning, and team management. Managers might spend part of their day at a client site, overseeing project progress and resolving any issues that arise. Back at the office, they review project deliverables, ensure compliance with standards, and mentor junior staff. Their role also includes strategic planning and business development, often working long hours, especially during crucial project phases. The ability to juggle multiple responsibilities and maintain strong client relationships is key to success in this role.

Senior Management and Leadership Roles

Senior Manager Senior managers take on higher-level responsibilities, including strategic planning, major client engagements, and cross-functional team leadership. They play a crucial role in business development and client retention.

Senior managers are deeply involved in the strategic aspects of projects and client management. Their day might start with high-level strategy meetings with senior leadership, followed by client presentations to secure new business or discuss major projects. They also oversee multiple projects, ensuring they stay on track and meet client expectations. Senior managers mentor managers and senior associates, providing guidance on complex issues. Working hours can be unpredictable, with long days and occasional weekend work to meet critical deadlines or client needs.

Director/Principal At this level, professionals are heavily involved in shaping firm strategy, acquiring new business, and leading large, high-impact projects. Directors and principals are often seen as future partners.

Directors and principals are key strategic players in the firm. Their days are filled with executive meetings, high-level client negotiations, and strategic planning sessions. They oversee the most significant projects and ensure they align with the firm's long-term goals. Business development is a major focus, with time spent cultivating relationships with potential clients and exploring new market opportunities. Directors and principals also play a crucial role in mentoring senior managers and identifying future leaders. Their working hours can be extensive, often involving travel and after-hours commitments to meet the demands of their role.

Partner Reaching the partner level is a significant milestone, indicating a high degree of expertise, leadership, and contribution to the firm's success. Partners are responsible for overall firm management, significant client portfolios, and strategic decisions.

A partner's day is a blend of strategic leadership and client engagement. They start with firm-wide strategy meetings, setting the direction for the business and reviewing performance metrics. Much of their time is spent with top clients, negotiating contracts, and ensuring client satisfaction. Partners are also heavily involved in high-stakes business development, attending industry events, and forging key partnerships. Their role involves significant travel and long hours, often extending into evenings and weekends, reflecting the elevated level of responsibility and commitment required. Despite the demanding schedule, the role is highly rewarding, offering substantial influence over the firm's direction and success.

Specialized and Alternative Paths

Technical Expert/Specialist Roles Some professionals may choose to become technical experts in areas like cybersecurity, forensic accounting, or tax law, offering deep expertise rather than broad managerial oversight.

A technical specialist starts their day reviewing the latest developments in their field, such as new cybersecurity threats or changes in tax law. They work on specialized projects, providing deep technical insights and solutions that generalists might not. Their day includes collaborating with other teams to address specific client issues, conducting technical training for colleagues, and authoring detailed reports. While their hours can be demanding, especially when tackling urgent problems, their role is crucial for the firm's technical proficiency and client trust.

Internal Roles Opportunities also exist within the firms' internal departments such as human resources, IT, marketing, and training, allowing professionals to leverage their skills in different contexts. For example, a senior manager may also serve as the COO of a division, managing these responsibilities 'side-of-desk' in addition to their primary role.

A senior manager doubling as the COO of a division starts their day balancing their client-facing responsibilities with internal management tasks. They might begin with a client meeting to discuss ongoing projects, followed by a session with their internal team to review operational strategies and performance metrics. Throughout the day, they handle inquiries from both clients and internal staff, working on business development while also ensuring the division runs smoothly. This dual role often extends their working hours, as they need to address both external and internal demands effectively. However, the experience gained from such roles is invaluable for their professional development and the firm's success.

Pursuing Further Education and Certifications

In the fast-paced and competitive environment of the Big 4 firms, professional certifications and further education play a pivotal role in career advancement. These credentials not only enhance technical skills but also increase marketability, provide networking opportunities, and open doors to higher-level positions. Here's an overview of some key certifications that professionals in the Big 4 might pursue:

Chartered Accountant (CA)

Recognized internationally, the CA designation is valuable for accountants working in different regions and sectors. It signifies a high level of expertise in accounting, finance, and business management. CAs often hold senior positions in accounting firms, corporations, and public sector organizations.

Benefits:

- Enhances credibility and professional standing.
- Provides in-depth knowledge of financial reporting, audit, and tax.
- Opens doors to leadership roles in various industries.

Typical Career Path:

Many CAs start their careers in public accounting, gaining experience in audit, tax, and advisory services. Over time, they may transition into senior roles such as financial controllers, CFOs, or even CEOs.

Certified Internal Auditor (CIA)

The CIA certification is beneficial for those specializing in internal audit, providing a deeper understanding of internal controls, risk management, and auditing processes. It is recognized globally and is often required for senior internal audit roles.

Benefits:

- Validates expertise in internal audit and risk management.
- Increases opportunities for higher positions within internal audit functions.
- Provides a comprehensive framework for auditing and risk assessment.

Typical Career Path:

CIAs often begin as internal auditors, progressing to roles such as audit manager, internal audit director, or chief audit executive. They may also work in risk management or compliance roles within various organizations.

Certified Information Systems Auditor (CISA)

Ideal for professionals in IT audit, information security, and risk management, the CISA certification demonstrates knowledge in auditing information systems, control, and assurance. It is a globally recognized certification offered by ISACA.

Benefits:

- Recognizes expertise in IT governance and audit.
- Enhances opportunities in IT audit, information security, and risk management.
- Provides a structured approach to assessing and mitigating IT risks.

Typical Career Path:

CISAs typically work in roles such as IT auditors, information security analysts, or IT risk managers. They may advance to positions like IT audit manager, chief information security officer (CISO), or IT risk director.

Chartered Institute of Management Accountants (CIMA)

The CIMA qualification is tailored for management accountants, focusing on strategic business management and financial strategy. It is recognized globally and highly valued in the corporate sector.

Benefits:

- Develops skills in financial strategy, risk management, and business performance.
- Opens up career opportunities in management accounting and financial leadership.
- Provides a global perspective on business and finance.

Typical Career Path:

CIMA professionals often start in roles such as management accountants or financial analysts. They can progress to senior positions like financial controllers, finance directors, or CFOs, and are often involved in strategic decision-making processes within organizations.

Other Technology-Related Qualifications

As technology continues to transform the business landscape, various other certifications are becoming increasingly relevant, particularly for professionals in the Big 4 who focus on IT, cybersecurity, and data analytics.

Certified Information Security Manager (CISM)

The CISM certification, also offered by ISACA, is geared towards management, focusing on managing and overseeing an enterprise's information security program.

Benefits:

- Validates expertise in information security governance, risk management, and incident management.
- Enhances career opportunities in IT security management.
- Recognized globally, particularly in leadership roles in IT security.

Typical Career Path:

CISM holders often work in roles such as information security managers, IT risk managers, and security consultants. They can advance to senior positions like CISO, IT director, or security operations director.

Certified in Risk and Information Systems Control (CRISC)

CRISC, another ISACA certification, focuses on enterprise IT risk management. It is ideal for professionals who design and manage an organization's risk management program.

Benefits:

- Recognizes expertise in identifying and managing IT risk.
- Enhances opportunities in risk management and IT governance.
- Provides a comprehensive framework for risk assessment and mitigation.

Typical Career Path:

CRISC professionals often start in roles such as IT risk analysts or IT compliance officers. They can progress to positions like risk managers, IT governance directors, or chief risk officers.

Certified Data Privacy Solutions Engineer (CDPSE)

CDPSE certification is offered by ISACA and focuses on the implementation of privacy solutions and data protection best practices.

Benefits:

- Recognizes expertise in data privacy and protection.
- Enhances career opportunities in data privacy, compliance, and security.
- Provides a framework for building and implementing privacy solutions.

Typical Career Path:

CDPSE holders often work in roles such as data privacy officers, compliance officers, and security consultants. They can advance to senior positions like chief privacy officer or head of data protection.

Leadership Development Programs

Leadership development is a cornerstone of career progression in the Big 4 firms. These programs are designed to identify and cultivate the next generation of leaders, providing them with the tools and experiences needed to excel in their careers. Here's an overview of the key components of leadership development within the Big 4:

Formal Leadership Programs

Many Big 4 firms have structured leadership development programs that identify and nurture high-potential employees. These programs often include partnerships with top business schools, offering courses and workshops that focus on advanced leadership skills, strategic management, and innovative thinking.

Examples of Leadership Programs:

Harvard Business School Executive Education This program offers a comprehensive suite of leadership development courses. Key areas of focus include negotiation skills, strategic decision-making, and organizational leadership. For a career at a Big 4 consulting firm, these courses can be instrumental. For instance, negotiation skills can help you secure better terms for your clients, while strategic decision-making can assist in providing high-level advice to businesses. The organizational leadership course can prepare you to lead teams effectively, a crucial skill in the consulting world.

Wharton School of the University of Pennsylvania Wharton is renowned for its leadership programs that emphasize global business perspectives, innovation, and financial acumen. These programs can provide you with a broad understanding of global markets, which is invaluable when advising multinational clients. The emphasis on innovation can help you bring fresh, creative solutions to your clients' problems. Additionally, the focus on financial acumen can enhance your ability to analyse financial statements and understand the financial implications of strategic decisions, a key requirement in consulting roles.

INSEAD Leadership Development Programme This program focuses on building leadership capabilities through experiential learning, peer coaching, and international networking. The experiential learning approach allows you to learn by doing, which can accelerate your understanding and mastery of leadership concepts. Peer coaching provides an opportunity to learn from others' experiences and perspectives, fostering a collaborative learning environment. The international networking aspect of the program can help you build a diverse network of professionals, which can be beneficial for future consulting engagements.

Participants in these programs gain exposure to cutting-edge business theories, real-world case studies, and practical leadership exercises. This training is complemented by opportunities to apply these skills in their roles within the firm.

Mentorship and Coaching

Access to mentors and executive coaches is a critical component of leadership development in the Big 4. These relationships provide guidance, support, and insights that help professionals navigate their career paths, overcome challenges, and achieve their career goals.

Benefits of Mentorship and Coaching

Personalized Career Guidance

Mentorship programs within the Big 4 firms offer invaluable personalized career guidance to professionals at all levels. Mentors, often seasoned veterans within the organization, provide mentees with insights and advice based on their own experiences navigating the complexities of the industry. These mentors help mentees identify their strengths, clarify their career goals, and develop a roadmap for success. Whether it's choosing the right client engagements, pursuing specialized certifications, or transitioning to leadership roles, mentors play a crucial role in helping mentees make informed career decisions that align with their aspirations and values.

Skill Development

Executive coaching, a cornerstone of professional development within the Big 4 firms, focuses on honing essential leadership skills. Coaches work closely with professionals to assess their strengths and areas for improvement, providing targeted feedback and strategies for skill enhancement. From refining communication techniques and mastering conflict resolution to cultivating strategic thinking and decision-making abilities, executive coaches help professionals develop the competencies needed to excel in their roles and advance their careers within the firm.

Networking Opportunities

Mentorship relationships often serve as gateways to expanded professional networks and new opportunities both within and outside the Big 4 firms. Mentors, with their extensive industry connections and insider knowledge, introduce mentees to key stakeholders, influential leaders, and potential collaborators. Through these connections, mentees gain access to exclusive networking events, industry conferences, and leadership development programs. Additionally, mentors may recommend mentees for high-profile projects, stretch assignments, or leadership roles, providing them with visibility and advancement opportunities within the organization. Beyond the firm, mentorship relationships may lead to introductions to potential clients, partners, or mentors in other industries, broadening mentees' horizons and opening doors to diverse career pathways.

> HAVING BEEN PART OF THE BIG 4 FOR SEVERAL YEARS, I'VE EXPERIENCED FIRSTHAND THE PROFOUND IMPACT OF MENTORSHIP ON MY CAREER DEVELOPMENT. WHAT SETS THE BIG 4 APART IS NOT JUST THE OPPORTUNITY TO BE MENTORED BUT ALSO THE CHANCE TO PAY IT FORWARD BY BECOMING A MENTOR MYSELF.
>
> BEING MENTORED HAS BEEN INSTRUMENTAL IN GUIDING MY CAREER TRAJECTORY, OFFERING INVALUABLE INSIGHTS, AND HELPING ME NAVIGATE THE COMPLEXITIES OF THE INDUSTRY. FROM PERSONALIZED CAREER ADVICE TO SKILL DEVELOPMENT AND NETWORKING OPPORTUNITIES, MY MENTORS HAVE PLAYED A PIVOTAL ROLE IN SHAPING MY PROFESSIONAL JOURNEY.
>
> HOWEVER, WHAT TRULY DISTINGUISHES THE BIG 4 IS ITS CULTURE OF RECIPROCITY, WHERE MENTORSHIP IS NOT JUST A ONE-WAY STREET BUT A TWO-WAY EXCHANGE OF KNOWLEDGE AND EXPERIENCE. AS I'VE PROGRESSED IN MY CAREER, I'VE HAD THE PRIVILEGE OF MENTORING JUNIOR COLLEAGUES, SHARING MY INSIGHTS, AND SUPPORTING THEIR GROWTH AND DEVELOPMENT.
>
> THE BENEFITS OF MENTORSHIP EXTEND BEYOND PERSONAL GROWTH; THEY RIPPLE THROUGHOUT THE ORGANIZATION, FOSTERING A CULTURE OF CONTINUOUS LEARNING, COLLABORATION, AND EXCELLENCE. AS A MENTOR, I'VE HAD THE OPPORTUNITY TO CONTRIBUTE TO THE SUCCESS OF OTHERS, BUILD MEANINGFUL RELATIONSHIPS, AND CULTIVATE A SENSE OF CAMARADERIE WITHIN MY TEAM.
>
> MOREOVER, MENTORING HAS SHARPENED MY LEADERSHIP SKILLS, DEEPENED MY UNDERSTANDING OF DIFFERENT PERSPECTIVES, AND REINFORCED MY OWN KNOWLEDGE AND EXPERTISE. BY GUIDING AND EMPOWERING OTHERS, I'VE BECOME A MORE EFFECTIVE LEADER AND A MORE VALUABLE ASSET TO THE FIRM.

Leadership Roles in Projects

Taking on leadership roles in client projects, internal initiatives, or professional networks is another vital aspect of leadership development. These opportunities allow professionals to build essential skills such as project management, strategic thinking, and team leadership.

Key Leadership Opportunities:

Client Projects Leading complex client engagements helps professionals develop strategic planning and problem-solving skills while managing diverse teams and client relationships.

Internal Initiatives Taking charge of internal projects, such as process improvements or new service development, enhances project management capabilities and fosters innovation.

Professional Networks Leading industry-specific networks or firm-wide committees builds visibility, influence, and collaborative skills.

International Assignments
Global Mobility Programs

At the heart of the Big 4 firms' commitment to fostering global talent lies their robust global mobility programs. These initiatives are designed to provide employees with unparalleled opportunities to immerse themselves in diverse cultures, navigate unfamiliar business landscapes, and broaden their professional horizons.

Short-term Assignments and Secondments

Short-term assignments and secondments represent a dynamic facet of the Big 4's global mobility programs. These opportunities, spanning from a few weeks to several months, offer professionals the chance to work on specific projects or client engagements in foreign offices. Whether it's assisting with a cross-border merger, conducting a regulatory compliance audit in a different jurisdiction, or supporting a multinational client's expansion strategy, short-term assignments provide hands-on experience in navigating the complexities of international business.

Long-term Relocations

For those seeking a deeper immersion in a different market, long-term relocations present an unparalleled opportunity for professional and personal growth. These assignments, often spanning one to several years, enable professionals to develop a comprehensive understanding of regional business practices, establish deep-rooted relationships with local stakeholders, and build a global network that spans continents. Whether it's leading a strategic initiative in an emerging market, spearheading a market entry strategy for a multinational corporation, or serving as a key liaison between regional offices, long-term relocations offer a transformative experience that transcends borders.

Benefits of International Experience

Broadened Perspectives

One of the most profound benefits of international assignments is the broadening of perspectives they afford. Working in diverse cultural and business environments exposes professionals to new ways of thinking, problem-solving, and collaborating. By navigating unfamiliar terrain, professionals develop a heightened sense of adaptability, resilience, and cultural intelligence, enabling them to thrive in an increasingly interconnected world.

Enhanced Client Relationships

International experience equips professionals with the knowledge, insights, and cultural sensitivity needed to forge deeper connections with global clients. By understanding the nuances of different markets, anticipating cross-cultural communication challenges, and tailoring solutions to meet local needs, professionals can deliver unparalleled value to clients operating in complex, multinational environments. Moreover, the ability to seamlessly navigate international business landscapes instils confidence and trust in clients, strengthening long-term relationships and positioning the firm as a trusted advisor on the global stage.

Career Advancement

Demonstrating the ability to thrive in international settings can be a catalyst for career advancement within the Big 4 firms. Firms highly value the versatility, adaptability, and cross-cultural competencies gained through international experience, recognizing them as essential qualities of future leaders. Whether it's accelerating progression through the ranks, assuming leadership roles on global initiatives, or being entrusted with high-impact client engagements, professionals with international experience are poised for success in today's interconnected business environment. In essence, international assignments serve as a springboard for career advancement, propelling professionals to new heights of leadership and influence within the firm and beyond.

Conclusion

Career growth and development within the Big 4 firms are marked by structured progression, continuous learning, and diverse opportunities. By understanding the long-term career paths, pursuing further education and certifications, and embracing leadership and international assignments, professionals can build a rewarding and impactful career. These firms offer a dynamic environment where ambition, adaptability, and a commitment to excellence can lead to significant personal and professional achievements.

Afterword

Congratulations on completing this journey through the intricacies of securing a position within the prestigious Big 4 firms in London. Whether you're just starting your career or seeking advancement opportunities, navigating the hiring landscape and understanding the nuances of these esteemed organizations can be both exciting and challenging.

Throughout this book, we've delved into various aspects of the Big 4 hiring process, from understanding the culture and values of these firms to crafting standout applications, mastering interviews, and thriving in a diverse workplace environment. Each chapter has provided valuable insights, practical tips, and actionable strategies to help you position yourself as a top candidate and excel in your professional endeavours.

Remember, landing a dream job at a Big 4 firm is not just about showcasing your technical skills and qualifications; it's also about embodying the core values, adapting to the cultural landscape, and demonstrating your potential for long-term growth and development within the organization.

As you embark on your journey, keep in mind the importance of continuous learning, networking, and personal growth. Stay adaptable, embrace diversity, and seize every opportunity to showcase your talents and capabilities. Your journey with the Big 4 firms is not just about reaching a destination but about embracing the challenges, seizing the opportunities, and shaping your career in a dynamic and rewarding industry.

Best of luck on your path to success, and may your journey with the Big 4 be filled with growth, fulfilment, and endless possibilities.

Warm regards,

Marc

www.ingramcontent.com/pod-product-compliance
Lightning Source LLC
Chambersburg PA
CBHW070350230526
45471CB00006B/2496